MANAGERIAL ACCOUNTING CHANGES FOR THE 1990s

John Y. Lee

McKay Business Systems

HF
5657.4
.L43
1987

McKay Business Systems

Copyright © 1987 by John Y. Lee.

ISBN 0-9617977-0-3

Library of Congress Catalog Card No. 87-60120

Printed in the United States of America

Publisher

McKay Business Systems
P.O. Box 597
Artesia, California 90702-0597
U.S.A.

ii

PREFACE

This book is concerned with the recent developments in U.S. industry and their impact on managerial accounting. The developments include fierce competition from overseas, top managers' responsive behaviors, influences of Japanese management practices and production methods, and advances in manufacturing technology.

For the last two years, the author has tried to incorporate the implications of these developments into cost and managerial courses. Moderate coverage of these issues was made in the undergraduate courses while in the graduate courses, the coverage was much more extensive.

The discussion of these developments has made the classroom instruction more lively and realistic. Student responses have been overwhelmingly positive. Above all, the instructor has felt better because something could be done to have students exposed to the realities of the industry, which many academics have felt lacking in our managerial accounting education.

Although the intention was noble, the actual discussion of these developments in the classroom required the reading of many articles from a wide variety of journals and practitioners' reports. Assimilation and reading of all the articles was a very time-consuming process and difficult tasks for both the students and the instructor.

That experience has prompted the author to write this book. Since this is one of the few undertakings of its kind in the cost and managerial accounting area, there were many problems. Among them, the lack of a suitable framework which would help integrate various suggested ideas and practical solutions was the most serious.

The author has tried to overcome this major difficulty by structuring the discussions in this fashion: 1) The developments were classified as those that affect product costing systems and controls; 2) the developments that influence performance measurement and other aspects of management control systems; and 3) the developments which can be classified as special topics.

In addition, an attempt was made in the area of performance measurement to construct a new way of looking at management control related to performance evaluation. The concept of positive performance is employed to explain the developments in the new environment.

It is hoped that this small project will help accounting professors and their students in their endeavor to study the current developments in industry and perhaps more important, what is likely to happen in the environment of the 1990s. For practitioners in the industry, this book could be used to help them integrate those pieces of information and obtain an overall perspective of ongoing and expected changes.

I am indebted to numerous individuals who provided help and encouragement in bringing this work to completion. I am especially grateful to Bart P. Hartman for providing helpful comments and suggestions during the preparation of the manuscript. In addition, I would like to express my appreciation to Yasuhiro Monden, a good friend of mine and the author of *Toyota Production System,* for giving me a valuable exposure to an entirely new way of thinking; to Sue Shochat for the collection of some very interesting cases; to J.Y. Jeon for his assistance in various stages of the work; and to Ron Milne for providing valuable support in the final stage of my writing. I also thank my present and former colleagues for their influence, support, and encouragement which have been so valuable thus far.

Finally, I wish to thank my wife, Jungmi, and my two children, Patti and Hanie, for their support and encouragement. Their love and unselfishness made this project a very pleasant one for me.

J.Y.L.

CONTENTS

CHAPTER 4:

Changing Technology and Its Impact on U.S. Industry 33

CHAPTER 5:

The Influences of the Changing Environment on Product Costing Systems and Control 47

CHAPTER 6:

The Influences of the Changing Environment on Management Control and Performance Measurement 63

CHAPTER 7:

CHAPTER ONE

The New Environment of Managerial Accounting

1-1. FORCES FOR CHANGE

A firm's cost accounting and management control systems should be designed and operated to provide information useful for managers' planning and control decisions. When the manager's decision environment changes considerably, the managerial accounting system needs to be updated and modified accordingly to accommodate the new, different informational needs.

In the last decade, U.S. managers have been awakened to the formidable challenges from (1) their overseas counterparts in domestic and international markets and from (2) technological changes including automation. With their substantially superior manufacturing performance as a basis, foreign competitors have increased their market share to a considerable extent in various industries — steel, automobile, and electronics, to name just a few.

U.S. industry, threatened by the challenges, have been analyzing and studying the competition, primarily the Japanese, in an effort to find answers to the operating and management problems faced by them. While some have attributed the Japanese success to their culture and unique business environment, many have concluded that the Japanese developed innovative operating methods and management practices, most of which can be transferred to the U.S. environment.

The realization of the problems and promises has led many innovative firms in various industries to come up with the decision to adopt new techniques — such as Just-in-time, total quality control, flexible manufacturing system, CAD/CAM, CIM, etc. — to improve their productivity and competitive strength. Following their lead, many other firms are joining the group. The overwhelming evidence thus far suggests that the firms that do not respond to the challenge will not survive in the environment of the 1990s or at best will face a marginal existence.

The consequences of the heavy international and technological influences on U.S. industry have been significant. Some industry leaders and scholars have even called the effects revolutionary. As U.S. industry — the environment of managerial accounting — undergoes the changes, the demands for new managerial accounting systems are ever increasing.

In the following chapters, the changing environment and its managerial accounting implications will be discussed. For management accountants, understanding the nature and realities of the new environment in which they must operate is a prerequisite to performing their role of designing and implementing a new managerial accounting system.

1-2. THE PROBLEMS OF U.S. INDUSTRY

Preoccupied with short-term profits which have been the primary measure used for performance evaluation, U.S. managers have largely ignored the long-term health of the firm. This has led to declines in productivity and has weakened competitive strength in both domestic and international markets.

There are many factors, of course, other than U.S. managers' preoccupation with short-term performance, that are responsible for the weakened condition of U.S. business. Most frequently cited causes for the malaise are: complex government regulations, deficiencies in government tax and monetary policies, and the energy price escalation by OPEC and concomitant high inflation of the 1970s.

According to Hayes and Abernathy [1980], nevertheless, these other causes "do not explain why the rate of productivity growth in the U.S. has declined both absolutely and relative to that in Europe and Japan." Nor do they explain why in many high-tech as well as mature industries the U.S. has lost its leadership position.

What are the underlying factors attributing to the decline in competitiveness of U.S. business? A review of various studies in this area indicates eight frequently cited reasons: 1) greater dependence of diversified corporations on short-term financial measurements such as return on investment (ROI) for evaluating managers' performance; 2) an increase in excessively cautious management behavior characterized by an unwillingness to assume even reasonable risk; 3) customer-oriented behavior of managers that has largely ignored innovative product and process development; 4) the lag in R & D investment and capital spending; 5) stock market myopia and managers' concern about sustaining stock price and avoiding takeover threat; 6) short tenure and high mobility of managers; 7) insignificant amount of long-term compensation compared to short-term compensation; and 8) difficulty in identifying the interests of a diverse set of stockholders.

Some of these are related to each other and intertwined. A more detailed analysis of these will be presented in Chapter 2.

1-3. U.S. INDUSTRY'S RESPONSE TO FOREIGN COMPETITION

The September 2, 1985, issue of FORTUNE reported that General Motors announced it had chosen Spring Hill, Tennessee, as the site for Saturn, a new auto company established to meet Japanese competition. GM reportedly was anxious to keep the new facility which will be managed in Japanese style, a safe distance from other GM plants, where antimanagement attitudes still run strong. Perhaps symbolically, the closest auto plant is 35 miles to the north, where Nissan Motor Co. operates its nonunion plant in "no nonsense" Japanese style. What are the implications of this report?

Confronted with the Japanese challenge, many forward-looking U.S. corporations have begun to make some drastic changes in their management practices and corporate operations. Now the necessity of initiating innovative improvements in corporate management seems to be felt by most businesses. Even the major automakers have adopted the Just-in-time and total quality control concepts that have subsequently saved hundreds of millions of dollars and have improved product quality. Saturn is just one more example of the recent innovative improvements that U.S. industry has introduced based on the lessons from the Japanese experience.

It is true that some attribute the superior manufacturing performance of Japanese firms to the unique culture and philosophy, thereby limiting the relevance and transferability of Japanese management practices to the U.S. But, according to Kaplan [1983], "many of the successful practices in Japan require only a management commitment to improve manufacturing performance through procedures and investments" that can be easily transferred to U.S. firms [p.687]. Kaplan cites the following examples:

- Ford was able to reduce overall inventories by $750 million, reducing inventory carrying costs by about $250 million a year, through a better coordination of its deliveries from suppliers.
- A Matsushita plant in the U.S. increased production volume by 40 percent while reducing defects from 150 per 100 sets produced to 3 over an 8-year period. They have bought this plant from Motorola and have kept essentially the same work force. In the Japanese parent company, the defect rate is 0.5 per 100 sets produced.

1-4. U.S. INDUSTRY'S RESPONSE TO CHANGING TECHNOLOGY

Advances in computer technology have made the dream of a fully automated factory something close to a reality. Now the automation technology in the U.S. is well on its way to realizing the concept of computer-integrated manufacturing (CIM). If CIM is installed by a company, the following will be made possible:

- Design a product using a computer-assisted design (CAD) system.
- Use a computer-assisted engineering (CAE) system to test the design.
- Make the product through a computer-assisted manufacturing (CAM) system that employs computer-controlled machine tools, robots, and other automated equipment.

The system will also be able to communicate with other systems such as manufacturing resource planning (MRP II) and manufacturing process planning (MPP) that help the company optimize the use of materials and other resources, and schedule production for optimum results, respectively.

Although perfecting the CIM concept in practice is yet to materialize, a considerable portion of the idea is already a reality. A flexible manufacturing system (FMS), which employs machine tools, robots, etc. under the integrated control of a mainframe computer, has already been installed at about 50 U.S. companies.

The availability of FMS — and eventually CIM — will bring fundamental changes to U.S. industry in many ways: The factory will become so flexible that it will be able to (1) produce a test copy of a product at a trivial cost; (2) changeover from one production run to another in a few minutes or seconds; and (3) adapt to changing market preferences on a very short notice.

Accordingly, companies will be able to produce to the order, rather than basing production on pure forecasts. This will shorten lead time and reduce inventory requirements dramatically. The automated factory will also require a reduced labor input, thereby providing U.S. companies with a competitive advantage over foreign counterparts.

With those benefits of automation, what prevents U.S. companies from making the investment?

There are many reasons ranging from a shortage of qualified manufacturing engineers to difficulty in justifying the cost of the investment. Perhaps the greatest factor is top management's basic tendency to avoid making long-term commitments because of the pressures of short-term performance evaluation.

Most agree, nevertheless, that the changes are coming. In the 1990s, it will be very difficult for a company using conventional manufacturing processes and equipment to compete with an automated competitor. To survive, companies will have to follow the lead of those innovative ones who have already made changes.

1-5. SUMMARY

In this chapter, a brief introduction to the changing environment of cost accounting and management control systems was provided. U.S. manufacturers are learning from their overseas counterparts, the Japanese in particular, that some drastic changes must be made in their way of thinking and management practices. Unless U.S. manufacturers make a long-term commitment by introducing new techniques developed in the U.S. and overseas, they may end up losing the international competition of the 1990s.

Fortunately, this realization has led many industry leaders to adopt new production, quality control, and inventory management techniques. As American firms make significant changes in the above areas and in other related operations such as purchasing, delivery, and transportation, management accountants must accommodate the changes by designing new managerial accounting systems to measure and evaluate operating performance.

In Chapter 2, an in-depth analysis of U.S. industry and the manager's environment will be made. This will help us understand the background of all the changes that have been made and those that will be made in the 1990s.

REFERENCES

Hayes, R.H., and W. J. Abernathy, "Managing Our Way to Economic Decline," *Harvard Business Review* (July-August 1980), pp.67-77.

Kaplan, R.S., "Measuring Manufacturing Performance: A New Challenge for Managerial Accounting Research," *The Accounting Review* (October 1983), pp.686-705.

SUGGESTED ADDITIONAL READINGS

Business Week, "How Automation Could Save the Day" (March 3, 1986), pp.72-74.

Lee, J.Y., "The Quiet Revolution in Inventory Management," *FE: The Magazine for Financial Executives* (December 1985), pp.37-40.

McConnell, C.R., "Why is U.S. Productivity Slowing Down?"*Harvard Business Review* (March-April 1979), pp.36-60.

Murrin, T., "Rejecting the Traditional Ways of Doing Business" (Chicago: American Production and Inventory Control Society, October 1982).

Takeuchi, H.,"Productivity: Learning from the Japanese," *California Management Review* (Summer 1981), pp.5-19.

CHAPTER TWO

U.S. Industry, Managers' Performance, and Incentives

2-1. U.S. INDUSTRY'S PROBLEMS

Why is U.S. industry having such difficulty meeting the challenges of overseas competition and changing technology? What are the underlying weaknesses of U.S. industry? What have caused those weaknesses?

An Analysis of the Problems

Most blame general economic forces. The long-term solution to the problems, however, may not be correctable simply by changing our government's tax laws, monetary policies, and regulatory practices, according to Hayes and Abernathy [1980].

Success in most industries these days, they charge, requires an organizational commitment to compete over the long run by offering superior products. Yet U.S. managers have increasingly directed their attention to short-term cost reduction and the management principles that prize analytical detachment.

In their analysis, Hayes and Abernathy give three primary reasons for the current problems:

1. As more companies decentralize their operations, they tend to rely on objectively quantifiable short-term financial measurements like return on investment

(ROI) for evaluating the performance of profit centers and individual managers. The "managerial remote control" like this produces an environment in which no manager can afford even a temporary dip in the bottom-line measure. This does not encourage innovation, the lifeblood of any vital firm.

2. In diversified corporations, managers lacking hands-on experience and concerned mainly with finance and control, are unwilling to assume even reasonable risk. They tend to be extremely cautious in allocating resources.

3. In the past, U.S. industry has learned that businesses should be customer oriented rather than product oriented. This has led to the following phenomenon: "Stop marketing makeable products and make marketable products." Deferring to a market-driven strategy is opting for customer satisfaction and lower risk in the short run at the expense of the development of superior products in the future.

The above analysis seems to be in line with those of Kaplan [1985] and Rappaport [1978].

Manufacturing Performance and Industry Strength

The problems in U.S. industry arose during the 1960s and 1970s when manufacturing was not considered a major part of corporate strategy [Kaplan, 1985]. Corporate emphasis shifted to producing earnings through mergers and acquisitions, or through attractive financing arrangements in debt markets, thus distracting attention from developing new products and processes.

Overseas competitors, in the meantime, continued to pay attention to their manufacturing operations. The Japanese, in particular, placed heavy emphasis on product and process development and came up with some extremely innovative production methods. (See Chapter 3 for the details of these methods.)

In most U.S. companies, production is not always the optimal career path leading to the top as compared to the financial and legal areas. This is reflected in the compensation scale as well. "MBAs becoming financial consultants are paid like quarterbacks, whereas, MBAs in manufacturing are paid like offensive linemen" [Corporate Accounting, 1985, p.14]. This tendency has contributed to the decline in the competitive strength of U.S. industry in domestic and international markets.

2-2. THE VIEW AND BEHAVIOR OF MANAGERS

Many of U.S. industry's problems discussed so far can be attributed to the lack of long-term commitment from corporate executives. Why do managers have such short-term view? Rappaport [1978] uses agency theory to explain the view and behavior of managers in his oft-quoted article on motivation of managers and corporate growth.

According to the Agency Theory

Rappaport provides the following explanation:

Under the theory of the behavior of principals (stockholders) and agents (managers), agents are employed by principals to manage the firm. Where principals have imperfect control over their agents, the agents may not always act in the best interests of the principals. Agents have their own interests and it may sometimes pay them to sacrifice the others' interests. In large corporations where it is difficult to identify the interests of so many different stockholders, managers tend to behave to maximize their economic interests and psychological satisfaction from self-actualization, esteem, and power.

In an agency setting, therefore, a moral hazard problem arises. This problem is concerned with the agent's self-interest-maximizing behavior at the expense of the principals. Actual behavior of managers takes the form of risk-reward tradeoffs in decision making, and sometimes, even management fraud.

Risk-Reward Tradeoffs

According to Fortune [1984], more than 70 percent of S & P 400 companies use the progress of earnings per share (EPS) as the primary measure of evaluating top management's performance. This, combined with the relatively short tenure of U.S. top-level managers, contributes to their preoccupation with short-term profits.

If performance evaluation is based primarily on EPS, managers tend to focus their attention on short-term results, avoiding risk-carrying projects that are healthy in the long run but reduce short-term profits. Examples of this nature are: R & D, personnel development, consumer relations, and other strategic programs.

When short-run financial operations are emphasized at the expense of increasing efficiency and effectiveness in manufacturing operations, management behavior adapts to the situation. One outcome is earnings manipulation.

Market Efficiency and Earnings Manipulation

To make short-term profits appear robust, managers often manipulate earnings. Most managers "prefer to report earnings that follow a smooth, regular, upward path" [Worthy, 1984].

Among manipulation techniques, accounting changes - change in accounting method and change in estimate[1] have the greatest and most permanent impact on earnings, Worthy states. Accounting changes are also the most recognizable since changes are disclosed in the notes to the financial statements.

But under the efficient market hypothesis [EMH], the wisdom of making accounting changes is questionable. Early tests of the effect on stock price of accounting changes [Ball, 1972; Sunder, 1975] indicate that stock price does not react to accounting changes, except those changes which affect income taxes.

EMH evidence indicated that investors are not fooled by higher earnings that do not bring additional cash flow to the firm, provided the accounting changes made are disclosed. Why, then, do firms keep making discretionary accounting changes?

A review of the literature on the subject provides the following answers:

1. Accounting changes have economic consequences if the changes alter the distribution of firms' cash flows, or the wealth of parties who use accounting earnings for contracting or decision making. Most management compensation plans

---

[1] Examples of change in accounting method are: LIFO-FIFO switches, changing the method of accounting for investment tax credit, revenue recognition, overhead, etc. Change in estimate can be seen in pension expense calculation (actuarial assumption change), depreciation expense calculation (change in the life of depreciable assets), and so forth.

are based on accounting net income or a rate of return on the book value of the investment. Accordingly, management's wealth can be affected by accounting changes, provided that the compensation plan is not adjusted to offset the changes.

2. Wall Street's widely-held belief is that managers pay more heed to the accounting consequences of major decisions than to the economics. According to Worthy, EMH researchers "don't realize that the higher earnings are embedded for infinity, but Wall Street forgets about the accounting change after a couple of years" [p.52].

2-3. INCENTIVE SYSTEM AND PERFORMANCE

Thus far, we have observed the problems of relying on short-term financial measures of performance in the design of managers' incentive plans. Then why do firms still rely so heavily on financial measures rather than operating measures more consistent with the long-term health of the firm?

The reason: Financial measures, such as earnings per share, provide a comprehensive measure of performance which is easy to understand. By denominating all operating and performance measures in dollars, firms can aggregate across diverse operating units to calculate an overall performance measure [Kaplan, 1983].

Recently, the growing concern over the problems of the incentive system based solely on short-term financial measures has led many firms to install new long-term incentive programs. According to Louis [1984], about 200 out of Fortune 500 companies have adopted performance-based long-term incentives.

In general, these programs offer fixed amounts of cash and stock if the executive manages the company to achieve certain financial goals over a period of three to five years. Unfortunately, financial goals that these companies use to measure their performance are primarily expressed in earnings per share figures. As discussed in section 2-2, the use of EPS fails to provide managers with proper motivation.

In addition to using a bogus performance measure such as EPS, these long-term incentive programs have another weakness: Most of them are "simply tacked onto traditional compensation packages" that pay bonuses for short-term performance. Since, at most companies, bonuses for short-term performance are larger than the payments from the long-term incentive program, executives tend to stress short term strategies to maximize their incomes. For example, at Holiday Inns, the chief executive's 1983 short-term bonus was about $600,000, compared to the annual payout from the long-term incentive program of $46,000. In this type of system, executives have relatively little incentive to concentrate on the long-term health of the company.

To make the long-term incentive programs work as intended, some have suggested the use of the stock price of the firm relative to others, instead of earnings figure, to measure the managerial performance. But, in reality, "managers as a breed just don't trust the stock market enough to base their incentive plans even on relative performance, and directors as a breed seem too unconcerned to prod management in this direction [Louis, p.65]."

2-4. QUESTIONS ON CORPORATE OWNERSHIP

A firm's success in most industries these days comes from an organizational commitment to compete over the long run by offering superior products. The current executive incentive systems, in general, do not provide proper motivation to the managers in that direction.

In order to maximize their own interests, U.S. managers have found that they need to pay close attention to short-term financial measures. Accordingly, not much efforts have been made to develop innovative products and production processes.

Then, what changes need to be made to correct the system on the industry level? Although this issue is not one that management accountants can deal with, it would be interesting to observe what solutions have been proposed by economists and management consultants.

Most proposals for change center on corporate ownership. Since most executives of large corporations own a small fraction of the company equity, the situation we have observed in this chapter is the natural consequence: They pursue their own interests, not those of the stockholders. And in order to insulate themselves from pressure to perform, they create a soft board of directors.

Binding the interests of executives and stockholders together tightly is the solution. To accomplish this, some suggest paying executives in corporate stock rather than in cash. Others, such as Peter Drucker, suggest the realignment of the relationship between investors and managers. They look to Japan as a working model.

Japanese companies rely more heavily on bank loans than do U.S. counterparts. The companies and banks work closely together, because banks have direct stakes in corporations which have to earn enough profits to make loan repayments on a continuing basis. This will lead the companies to strengthen their long-term competitiveness. The lenders do not put heavy pressure on borrowers to focus on short-term results, when the loans will be outstanding for a long-term period.

2-5. SUMMARY

In the new environment of the 1980s, U.S. industry is being challenged by competition from overseas, primarily Japan, to change its course. Understanding the underlying weaknesses of U.S. industry and the reasons for them is necessary for our study of managerial accounting implications of the various changes taking place presently and in the 1990s.

In this chapter, we have tried to focus these issues into several theoretical frameworks. Chapter 3 will be devoted to the subject of Japanese management practices and production methods which have exerted enormous influence on U.S. industry.

REFERENCES

Ball, R., "Changes in Accounting Technique and Stock Prices," *Empirical Research in Accounting: Selected Studies 1972, supplement to the Journal of Accounting Research* (1972), pp.1-38.

Corporate Accounting, "Cost Accounting: A Revolution in the Making - An Interview with R.S. Kaplan" (Spring 1985), pp.10-16.

Hayes, R.H., and W.J. Abernathy, "Managing Our Way to Economic Decline," *Harvard Business Review* (July-August 1980), pp.67-77.

Kaplan, R.S., "Measuring Manufacturing Performance: A New Challenge for Managerial Accounting Research," *The AccountingReview* (October 1983), pp.686-705.

Louis, A.M., "Business Is Bungling Long-Term Compensation," *Fortune* (July 23, 1984), pp.65-69.

Rappaport, A., "Executive Incentives vs. Corporate Growth,"*Harvard Business Review* (July-August 1978), pp.81-88.

Sunder, S., "Empirical Analysis of Stock Price and Risk As TheyRelate to Accounting Changes in Inventory Valuation," *The Accounting Review* (April 1975), pp. 305-315.

Worthy, F.S., "Manipulating Profits: How It's Done," *Fortune* (June 25, 1984), pp.50-54.

SUGGESTED ADDITIONAL READINGS

Cawly, R.H., "A Company Guide to Compensating Top Executives,"*Journal of Accountancy* (November 1985), pp.166-176.

Crystal, G.S., *Questions and Answers on Executive Compensation* (Englewood Cliffs, New Jersey: Prentice-Hall, Inc., 1984).

Ellig, B.R., *Executive Compensation — A Total Pay Perspective* (New York: McGraw-Hill Book Co., 1982).

Kaplan, R.S., "The Evolution of Management Accounting," *The Accounting Review* (July 1984), pp. 390-418.

Murphy, K.J., "Top Executives Are Worth Every Nickel They Get,"*Harvard Business Review* (March-April 1986), pp.125-132.

Poster, C.Z., "Executive Compensation: Taking Long-Term Incentives out of the Corporate Ivory Tower," *Compensation Review* (Second Quarter 1985), pp. 20-3.

Scotese, P.G., "From the Board Room: Fold up Those Golden Parachutes," *Harvard Business Review* (March-April 1985), pp.168-171.

CHAPTER THREE

International Influences on U.S. Management Practices

3-1. THE INITIAL "SHOCK"

U.S. manufacturers have followed the practice of accepting their production environment as given and implementing policies that are "optimal" with respect to these existing conditions [Kaplan, 1983, p.688]. The Japanese, in the meantime, have been almost obsessed with long-term planning and innovation in operations based on their management philosophy formulated since the 1950s.

U.S. executives who visit the plants of their competitors in Japan receive an initial shock when they see virtually zero inventory on the factory floor. In the U.S., a "reasonable level" of backup parts inventory on the factory floor has been accepted as a fact of life at manufacturing plants for a long time.

A further look into the manufacturing operations in the two countries reveals the following differences:[1]

---

[1] Compiled from Newsweek [October 28, 1985; p.62], Kaplan [1983], and Murrin [1982].

Ford

- Produces an average of 2 engines a day per employee
- The above production requires 777 sq. ft. of plant space
- Has up to 3 weeks of backup inventory

Toyota

- Produces an average of 9 engines a day per employee
- The above production requires 454 sq. ft. of plant space
- Has 1 hour of backup inventory

Chrysler

- About 500 in-plant job classifications

Toyota

- 7 in-plant job classifications

A Typical U.S. Auto Plant

- A changeover in the metal stamping of major parts from one model to another takes 6 hours

Toyota

- The same changeover takes 3-5 minutes

What do these differences mean? In terms of small car manufacturing costs, "Made in Japan" has the following cost edge against "Made in U.S.A.":[2]

	U.S.	Japan
Hourly labor	$1,500	$ 450
Salaried labor	500	250
Parts, materials, and services purchased	3,350	2,750
Depreciation, amortization, and utilities	500	300
Ocean shipping	—	400
Total	**$5,850**	**$4,150**
Difference	$1,700	

The above comparisons illustrate the weakened competitive strength of U.S. automobile industry even in the domestic market. This is one example, but similar observations can be made in many other industries.

Before we take a look at what U.S. industry is doing to remedy this situation, it is useful to examine how Japanese industry has been able to accomplish these results.

3-2. JAPANESE MANAGEMENT PRACTICES

Much of the success experienced by the Japanese can be attributed to the fact that many Japanese companies have developed management practices associated with high productivity and low turnover and absenteeism. Many factors go into the

---

[2] This comparison is taken from the estimate provided in Fisher [1985].

overall system of management in large Japanese firms, most of which are admittedly borrowed from the U.S. [McGovern, 1983]. It is the method in which these factors are blended and utilized that makes the Japanese philosophy work so effectively.

Emphasis on Human Resource Development

Possibly the most important underlying belief in most Japanese companies is that human resources are the firm's most important and profitable assets in the long run [Hatvany & Pucik, 1981].[3] The development of a management theory is built upon the premise of human resource development.

The underlying focus of developing the firm's human resources is supported by various strategies. Japanese style management stresses the importance of a strong commitment to total quality control, from the president of the company to the newest trainee. Ideally, this commitment to quality should include the employees of all customers and suppliers as well. This is coupled with a long-term perspective in Japan where employee development, evaluation, and reward systems are all designed with long-range goals in mind [Cope, 1982].

Job Security

A policy of lifetime employment helps create the kind of loyal work force that will be concerned with total quality control. The rule in large Japanese firms is to hire male employees after graduation from high school or college with the intent of retaining the employee for the rest of his working life. In essence, Japanese companies develop their own labor market internally.

Job security is assured during fluctuating economic conditions by using female and part-time employees. Flexibility is further achieved in times of recession by cutting salaries and bonuses instead of laying off full-time workers.

Japanese managers believe that job security improves morale and productivity, limits turnover and training costs, and increases the unity of the organization. Even poor performers are either retrained or transferred, and not simply dismissed. Firms in Japan invest much time and money in training. Skills which are learned on the job are largely company specific, thus discouraging interfirm mobility and limiting turnover.

A Unique Company Philosophy

Secure employment is a key factor for the effective implementation of other management strategies. One of these strategies is the articulation of a unique company philosophy. A philosophy that is stated and carried through presents a clear picture of the firm's objectives, norms and values. Knowledge of company goals gives direction to employees' actions. Understanding and supporting the philosophy brings the individual closer to the organization and to co-workers with shared objectives. These philosophies usually describe the firm as a family, distinct from

---

[3] While most examinations of Japanese management practices [JMP] concentrate on confirming or disconfirming the existence of supposedly unique characteristics of Japanese industry, Hatvany and Pucik look at JMP from an entirely different perspective: They present a model of JMP, that rests on fairly universal elements suitable for a comparative review. This provides an integrated perspective which is preferred to other analyses made in isolation from other structural and process variables.

any other firm. Heavy emphasis is usually placed on harmony, cooperation, and teamwork within the corporate family.

Harmony among Employees

A related strategy is the intensive socialization of employees. A primary function of the socialization process is to ensure that employees have understood the company's philosophy and seen it in action. This effort begins at the initial screening process, when recent graduates are being considered for employment.

The two basic criteria for hiring are moderate views and a harmonious personality. Because workers are expected to remain in a company for most of their careers, careful selection is necessary to ensure the hiring of those individuals most likely to fit well within the company's climate. The employee is assimilated during a training process designed to familiarize the worker with the various values and objectives of the firm. The individual is "resocialized" each time he enters a new position.

Job Rotation

The technique of job rotation teaches additional skills, and is part of a long-range, experience-building program through which the firm grooms its future managers. Holding positions in various functions and locations within the company gives the employee a better feel for the organization's overall needs. Job rotation is one of many techniques used by Japanese firms to attain the strategies discussed previously.

Related to job rotation is the concept of slow promotion. Promotion is slow, in part due to the lifetime employment strategy which limits upward mobility. This serves to encourage job rotation which produces individuals who become flexible generalists within a firm instead of specialists of a trade or task. Hiring from outside the company into upper-level positions is rare, so employees are more content to wait their turn, knowing that it will come eventually. Job rotation helps assure that the workers do not get bored or discouraged between promotions.

Evaluation and Promotion

Promotion systems in Japan tend to be two-fold. Promotion in "status" — for instance, from assistant vice president status to vice president status — is based on evaluations and seniority within the firm. Promotion in "position" — such as from deputy head to head of the production department — is based on evaluations and the availability of vacancies at a higher level. Not everybody who is promoted to vice president will assume the position of a department head.

The employee evaluation itself plays a major role in Japanese style management. Employee evaluations are usually conducted on an annual or semi-annual basis. The appraisal system is complex and includes not only performance measures, but also measures of desirable personality traits and behaviors such as, creativity, emotional maturity, and cooperation with others. In most companies, potential, personality and behavior, rather than output, are the key criteria. Team-level performance and cooperation are strongly emphasized [Ouchi and Jaeger, 1978].

No "Stars"

There is no room for "stars" in the Japanese system. It is felt that the dominant personalities of stars suppress creative thought in nonstars. This problem is avoided when filling a leadership position by promoting the consensus choice of subordinates and peers. This practice fosters team spirit and places individuals in leadership roles who have the respect and support of subordinates and peers as well as superiors [Cope, 1982].

Most company policies in Japan tend to be group oriented. Japanese organizations devote far greater attention to group motivation and cooperation than to that of individual employees. Tasks are assigned to groups, rather than individuals. The group is usually responsible for designing the method which is used to perform the task, thus stimulating team unity. Skills developed through job rotation prevent group production setbacks when workers are absent. Also, intergroup rivalry is often encouraged to stimulate constructive competition to the extent that does not hurt harmony within the company.

Quality Control Circles

One widely used group-based technique for discussing and solving problems is quality control circles. Quality control circles are designed to identify and handle a particular workshop's problem. Individuals from outside the group are only called in to educate the group in analytical problem solving or to provide specialized technical advice. Although certain limits and restrictions are placed on these groups by management, the quality control groups have significant leeway to provide motivation through direct employee participation in the design and improvement of the work process [Hatvany & Pucik, 1981].

Decision-Making Process

The extensive face-to-face communication in Japan has led to consultative decision-making. The usual procedure for management decision-making is that a proposal is initiated by a middle manager, often under the directive of top management. The middle manager will then discuss the proposal with peers and supervisors. When this group is familiar with the issues involved, a formal request for a decision is made. Because of the previous discussions, the proposal is almost inevitably agreed upon, often in a ceremonial group meeting [Hatvany and Pucik, 1981]. The manager will not usually implement the decision until others who will be affected have had sufficient time to offer their opinions and suggestions, and are willing to support the decision even though they may not be in total agreement.

In summary, the preceding management strategies and techniques are the primary components of what has become known as Japanese management theory or Japanese style management. Clearly, the concepts and practices involved are interrelated and work most effectively as elements of the entire system. It is a remarkably well-integrated system that serves the needs of individuals while achieving the goals of the organization.

How Much Can Be Transferred?

Japanese style management which has been described so far is the system as it exists ideally. It should be understood that usually only in the larger Japanese companies are most or all of these methods in existence. As will be discussed in more detail later in this chapter, certain of these techniques, such as lifetime employment, are more easily utilized by firms less vulnerable to recession.

There has been much research and discussion correlating the success of management in Japan and the Japanese culture. Studies have been conducted in which vast differences have been identified in the perception, leadership, organization, and motivation between the United States and Japan. These differences have been linked to culture.

However, many contend that the objectives and relationships upon which Japanese management philosophy is based are not unique to any one culture [Hatvany & Pucik, 1981]. In the wake of declining productivity in the United States, many American managers have turned their attention towards the management practices that are felt to have contributed to the Japanese success and have begun to adopt the ideas of the Japanese system with varying degrees of success.

Among the problems U.S. firms have experienced in their attempt to adopt some Japanese management practices was the failure to obtain the support of labor unions. Coordination with and the support of the unions are essential, since resistance from the local chapters of various craft unions will make some adopted practices ineffective. For example, at GM's Chevrolet plant in Adrian, Michigan, the first two attempts to make quality control (QC) circles work failed. The primary reason was management's failure to obtain the support of the local chapter of the United Auto Workers. QC circles at the Chevy plant had to compete with the union officials who felt that the circles would somehow assume some of their role as the workers' representative. The consideration for union support is not as serious in Japan because unions are company-based.

3-3. THEORY Z AND INNOVATIVE U.S. FIRMS

William Ouchi and his colleagues, based on their studies of some innovative and rapidly growing American firms, have found the following: Firms that believe in the trustworthiness of their employees, and demonstrate this in the employee relations will note marked improvements in employee morale and productivity. They call these firms Theory Z organizations [Ouchi and Jaeger, 1978; Ouchi and Johnson, 1978; Ouchi and Price, 1978]. The Theory Z organization has a basic similarity with the Japanese organization in that both place heavy emphasis on human resource development. But there are differences between the two as illustrated below.

	Theory Z	**Japanese**
Employment	Long-term	Lifetime
Basic responsibility	Individual-oriented	Group-oriented
Performance measures	Explicit	Implicit
Career and skill	Moderately specialized	Non-specialized

With these differences, the Theory Z organization still can develop a community of employees, which is compared to a family of employees the Japanese have tried to develop.

In the Theory Z organization, a strict profit center is not operated although the divisional profitability is calculated as a performance measure. Instead, division managers are guided by broad corporate objectives in their decision making, which might sometimes cause the divisional earnings to suffer. In this "community," the employees have subtlety in their understanding of one another's needs and objectives.

In order to promote the "Z-ness," a Theory Z organization must explicitly state subtle, complex, and long-run considerations to be made in decision making in a cogent and integrated statement of management philosophy. The management philosophy, then, must be properly interpreted and practiced through long-term employment, slow promotion after managers have had time to learn, and a performance evaluation system that reflects the complexity of the philosophy.

In the Type Z organization, departments extend assistance to one another and make short-run sacrifices for others, since everybody knows that they will be around for a sufficiently long time to get credit for what they have done for others.

This is in contrast to a typical U.S. firm, where managerial decisions are made on the basis of quantifiable, measurable criteria. There is a wide-spread notion that reducing complex and ambiguous realities to straightforward numbers represents the essence of rationality in administration. But, according to Ouchi[1981], with an employee turnover rate of about 24 percent a year, compared to 4 percent a year in Japan, many U.S. firms may be organizations of strangers. Here, the relationship, measurement, and control within the firm are so contractual, so straightforward, and so simple, that any stranger can instantly understand them.

The Theory Z, in essence, presents a blend of the American and the Japanese forms of management. In the next section, we will examine an example of the Japanese form of management practiced in the production environment.

3-4. TOYOTA PRODUCTION SYSTEM (KANBAN AND JUST-IN-TIME)

The Toyota production system, a forerunner of the innovative production practices in Japan, is a well-integrated system of interrelated production concepts and techniques. The fundamental goal of the system is to produce defect-free goods at the desired time, in the desired quantity, and at the lowest cost.

To accomplish the goal, Toyota has developed various operating concepts: Just-in-Time (JIT), Jidoka (autonomous control of defects),[4] and flexible work force.

Just-in-Time Production

JIT production is a concept that dictates every process to produce parts only when they are needed, and only in the quantity needed. This seemingly impossible task, when properly executed, can shorten production lead time (parts issued — products completed) and virtually eliminate unnecessary work-in-process and finished-goods inventories.

How does Toyota implement JIT production? There should be an information system that enables each process to be informed of what kinds of parts, when, and how many to produce.

---

[4] This interpretation of Jidoka was made by Monden [1983].

The medium used to accomplish that purpose is Kanban, a tag-like card attached to the part containers. When the parts in a container begin to be used, a worker in that process detaches the withdrawal Kanban attached to the container, and puts it in the withdrawal Kanban box. As the number of withdrawal Kanbans reaches the predetermined level, a worker takes the Kanbans and the empty containers to the store of the preceding process.

There he picks up the same quantity of parts represented by the withdrawal Kanbans, and replaces another type of Kanban (called production Kanban) attached to each container with the withdrawal Kanban he brought. These replaced production Kanbans are put in the production Kanban box, and are held there in sequence until they reach the predetermined level.

When the level is reached, they are picked up and used as production orders: The preceding process produces the same number of parts withdrawn by the subsequent process [Sugimori, Kusunoki, Cho and Uchikawa, 1977; Monden, 1983].

The produced parts and the production Kanbans are placed in the store of the preceding process allowing the subsequent process to withdraw them in the manner previously described.

As Figure 3.1 illustrates, the process described in this section takes place at every process of Toyota production, starting at the final assembly line and continuing through to the subcontractors' production lines.

Minimizing Inventory Level and the Number of Kanban

As shown in the preceding section, any withdrawal of parts requires the same number of Kanbans. Therefore, the minimization of inventory along the production

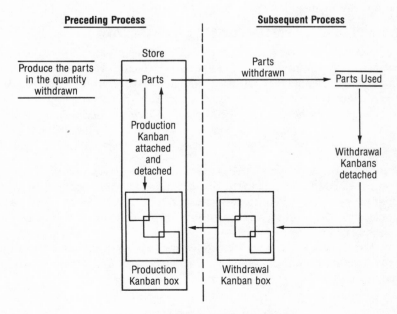

Figure 3.1. The Flow of Kanban and Parts.

processes is translated as the minimization of the number of Kanban in the implementation of the JIT production. Then, how does Toyota determine the number of Kanban?

Numerous articles published in the areas of industrial engineering and production research disclose the following formula which originally appeared in Toyota's internal manual:

$$n = \frac{Q(T_w + T_p)(1 + r)}{c}$$

where n = total number of Kanban,

Q = average demand quantity per day,

T_w = waiting time along the production lines,

T_p = time needed for processing and withdrawal of parts,

r = indicator of the inefficiency at the shop,

and c = container capacity.

When the size of Q, the average demand for parts per day, increases, the pressure to use more Kanbans builds up. This, nevertheless, does not lead to the automatic increase of **n**.

Toyota has cultivated its ability to deal with small changes in demand.[5] By reducing T_w (waiting time) and T_p (processing and withdrawal time), the frequency of Kanban movements is increased. This means all lines can smooth production level without adding more Kanbans to the existing flow.

The fact that the final assembly line initiates the production process is the key to the successful levelling of production. Only the final assembly line knows what the daily production sequence will be. Other processes along the line get the information on production requirements when they collect production Kanbans at their store. Adjustments to the production plan at the final assembly line will naturally be reflected along the rest of all the lines through the use of Kanban.

As a control policy, Toyota tries to keep the number of Kanban constant under normal conditions. As a result, to meet the increase in demand for parts, a shop must shorten the production and withdrawal time, and must improve efficiency in allocating workers. If the shop is incapable of increasing efficiency, it will see line-stops and/or will have to put in overtime.

This capability (or, more precisely, lack of it) of each shop is indicated by the value of r in the above formula. A shop incapable of making necessary improvements to adapt to the change in demand may have to increase the number of Kanbans for a certain period of time. It, of course, will have to live with a higher level of inventory and this apparent inefficiency will immediately be noticed by management.

The inverse relationship between **c**, the container capacity, and the number of Kanban is self-explanatory. If a plant uses bigger containers, it could handle the same production volume with fewer Kanbans.

---

[5] The "small" changes has been understood as a variation within a 10 percent range. When a substantial change in demand takes place, then the number of Kanban may have to be increased. This may also call for a rearrangement of the entire production process.

What if the demand decreases? From the formula, it is obvious that the production lead time, T_w and T_p, will accordingly be prolonged. The pace of the workers at the shop will also slow down. This will cause the plant to transfer some workers to other areas until the situation turns around [Kimura and Terada, 1981].

Autonomous Control of Defects (Jidoka)

While many U.S. firms are willing to accept an established level of defects (Acceptable Quality Level, or AQL), Japanese manufacturers have an entirely different attitude. Toyota, for example, has maintained the philosophy that no defect is acceptable. An enormous amount of attention is given to quality control which has made it possible that virtually no defective parts will flow through the system unnoticed.

At a Toyota plant, each worker can, and is required to, stop the line by pushing a button when his work is interrupted because of defective units withdrawn from the preceding process. Since only a minimal amount of work-in-process inventory is maintained, if the worker cannot repair the defective parts himself, the work is interrupted.

This line stoppage forces immediate attention to the problem and the cause is investigated. If the circumstances which led to the production of the defective unit can be determined, then preventive actions are taken to prevent the same type of defect from occurring again.

A worker can also stop the line when he cannot perform the standard operations routine within a given time. When this delay occurs, the worker next to him or the supervisor usually lends a hand to help him out. This system prevents poor-quality work due to insufficient time available to do the job.

The heavy reliance on workers' self-inspection at each process helps not only to prevent defective parts from reaching the final process, but also to reduce the number of full-time inspectors at the end of the line. The autonomous control of defects through workers' self-inspection has another distinctive advantage over the statistical quality control exercised by most U.S. firms:[6] Before the defect detected at the end of the line is studied and used as feedback information, the processes may produce many more defective units because of the time lag between the detection and correction of the defect. Thus, the on-the-spot correction is preferred to the conventional produce-and-rework-if-defective routine.[7]

Flexible Work Force and Multi-skill Workers

The strength of JIT is its flexibility in adapting to the changes in demand. When the pace at a shop slows down, excess work force is noticed immediately and workers are assigned to different jobs in the plant or other plants. To achieve the maximum possible flexibility in allocating workers to different jobs, Toyota has trained multi-skill workers. At a conventional assembly line, a worker performs primarily a

---

[6] Although the company-wide implementation of Jidoka has been made, statistical sampling is still used for lot production at Toyota on a limited scale.

[7] Production researchers have also argued that the zero defect approach leads to a substantial reduction in long-term manufacturing costs.

single function on a single machine or a few machines of the same type. Multi-skill workers perform different functions on various types of machines at the same time.

Toyota has been using U-shaped machine layout and job rotation to facilitate this process. As illustrated in Figure 3.2, a conventional layout allows workers to operate multiple machines of the same type. Although this multiple-machine layout improves efficiency by increasing output per worker compared to the one-machine-one-worker layout, it causes work-in-process inventory to accumulate between processes, for example, between stations M1 and M2. Since the jobs of two workers, W1 and W2, are not balanced (or levelled) through a method such as the JIT pull-through system, W1 could produce more than W2 needs sometimes.

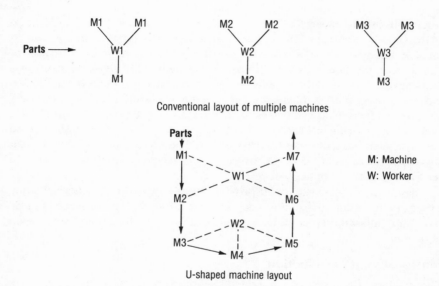

Conventional layout of multiple machines

M: Machine
W: Worker

U-shaped machine layout

Figure 3.2. Conventional vs. U-Shaped Machine Layout.

The U-shaped layout allows each process to produce only one unit, and to convey only one unit at a time between processes. This one-piece production and conveyance can take place, since one multi-skill worker operates several machines simultaneously. (For example, a worker, W1 in Figure 3.2, operates machines M1, M2, M6, and M7.)

As discussed in section 3-2, job rotation is practiced company-wide. Workers in a plant are rotated through almost every processing job in a shop for a period of time. This job rotation trains multi-skill workers who can be reassigned to any process when the need to adapt to changes in demand arises.

Small-Lot Deliveries from Suppliers

To accomplish JIT from the final assembly line down to the initial process, a close coordination with suppliers is also necessary. Large-lot deliveries of parts from suppliers will cause parts inventory to pile up, disrupting the whole system of

JIT. But can suppliers accommodate the needs of Toyota in the same manner as a preceding process does for a subsequent process in Toyota plants?

According to Monden [1983, p.36], Toyota had 98 percent of its suppliers implement the JIT concept by 1982. This report indicates that almost all suppliers could make deliveries as required by Toyota, although only 50 percent of them could employ the JIT method in their own production process. This leaves 48 percent of Toyota suppliers carrying the risk of stocking sufficient inventory of parts to meet Toyota's demand on time.

Toyota provides its suppliers with a monthly production plan, which is subject to change, about two weeks before the month the plan covers. Information on the actual demand for parts is relayed to the suppliers only hours before Toyota needs the parts.

For frequently used similar parts, Toyota employs the withdrawal Kanban (called the supplier Kanban): The suppliers produce the parts based on the Kanban they receive. The system works in this fashion. When the parts delivered are used at the Toyota assembly line, supplier Kanbans are detached. The empty boxes and these Kanbans are taken to the supplier's store by a truck. A second truck, loaded with boxes of parts with Kanbans attached, is already waiting there. The truck driver then switches trucks and drives the loaded truck to Toyota. The third truck, in the meantime, is being unloaded at Toyota. The driver comes in with the loaded second truck, switches trucks, and drives the third truck to the supplier. Involved in the delivery routine are: One truck driver, one worker unloading at Toyota, and another loading at the supplier's store.

For dissimilar, larger parts, Toyota provides suppliers with a sequence schedule that tells them the order of assembly; such as, Celica, Tercel, Corolla, Tercel, Celica, and so on. Suppliers would receive hourly information with a four-hour lead time on the sequence.

Conventional vs. JIT Production

The striking differences between the JIT production and the conventional production are summarized below:

1. To inform various processes of accurate timing and quantity of production:
   - Conventional - Provides monthly production schedules to every process including the final assembly line.
   - JIT - Does not provide simultaneous monthly production schedules to every process, only the final assembly line is informed.
2. To implement the production plan:
   - Conventional - The preceding process supplies the parts to the subsequent process (push-through system).
   - JIT - The subsequent process withdraws the parts from the preceding process. The final assembly line initiates (pull-through system).
3. Response to necessary adjustments in schedule because of product demand changes or production-related trouble at some point:
   - Conventional - Unable to respond promptly. Each process must adjust the schedule simultaneously. To compensate, it is necessary to hold backup inventory between processes.

• JIT - Can respond promptly. The final assembly line makes the adjustment and removes the parts it needs. The immediately preceding process then produces to replace only those parts withdrawn by the final assembly line. The same process takes place all the way down to the initial process, thus there is no need for backup inventory.

3-5. U.S. INDUSTRY'S RESPONSE

There has been ample evidence that Japanese management practices and production techniques, when properly implemented, increase productivity to a substantial degree. How, then, have American firms responded to the Japanese success with these methods? In hopes of improving their productivity in do-or-die situations, many U.S. firms have adopted the above-mentioned methods. Early results of the adoption indicate that most firms have been successful in their recent endeavors. Some of the firms, nevertheless, have found the implementation costly and disappointing.

By far, the technique which has been more popular than any other is JIT. U.S. manufacturers have learned the lesson that inventory is waste. They have realized that JIT is a concept which, when properly implemented, can drastically reduce inventory and the associated costs of holding inventory. Industries faced with ever increasing competition from Japan tend to have spearheaded the American conversion to JIT. The concept of JIT has been introduced in areas other than production as well, such as purchasing and transportation.

Since the implementation of JIT and other methods should be preceded by successful human resource management — the foundation for all other functional operations of a firm — substantial changes have also taken place in this area. In the following sections, we will examine what influences the new techniques have had on the environment of management accounting.

3-6. JIT PURCHASING AND PRODUCTION

Under the concept of JIT purchasing, a buyer is encouraged to buy from as few suppliers as possible, within close proximity of the buyer's facility. When General Motors made its commitment to JIT in 1982, the number of suppliers was to be eventually reduced by 50 percent. Suppliers were to be awarded long-term contracts, and single sources used whenever possible. This policy, according to Schonberger and Ansari[1984], strengthens buyer-supplier relationships and tends to result in a higher-quality product.

In Ypsilanti, Michigan, a GM assembly plant and a transmission plant are right across the street from each other, providing close proximity. GM's Hydramatic Division, which makes the transmissions, plans to institute JIT purchasing not only in Ypsilanti, but also in other GM assembly plants.

At GM's Buick City in Flint, Michigan, JIT is enhanced by a bar-coding system that helps maintain better control of the thousands of parts they handle. This seems to be Buick City's own version of Kanban. This plant does body stamping at the same location where the automobiles are assembled, and works with only an eight-hour supply of inventory [Forbes, 1984, p.13].

To help firms implement some of the same relations with their suppliers that the Japanese have arranged, primarily in controlling the rise in costs to the suppliers, the auto industry has established the Automotive Industry Action Group. This group is made up of representatives of automakers and suppliers throughout the auto industry. Its purpose is to study, for industry-wide adoption, various improvement measures and the Japanese production techniques[Heydt, 1984].

Westinghouse Electric has been using a JIT system at its Bloomington, Indiana, plant since 1981. Since then, parts inventory has been reduced by 45 percent, and plant stockouts were reduced by 95 percent. Previously, two stockouts a week were common, and resulted in "spot" purchases at premium prices [Industry Week, 1982, p.21].

The most famous among the decisions to adopt JIT probably has been that of General Motors on its Saturn project. As a new subsidiary of GM, Saturn will use a JIT inventory system. In addition, it will build engines, stamp bodies, and assemble finished cars in the same plant. Major subassemblies will be constructed by work teams who will be responsible for developing their own rules and procedures. GM hopes that the Saturn plant will serve as a prototype for its future facilities (Newsweek, 1985, p.56).

Saturn plant will practically be a laboratory of GM for production innovation, using a combination of new technology and old Japanese know-how. When the first Saturn car rolls out of the plant in 1990, it will embody every new cost-reducing method GM can find based on the JIT concept and sophisticated American technology.

Warner-Lambert, a manufacturer of products ranging from pharmaceuticals and consumer goods to candies, has applied the concept of JIT to its production processes. The major shift has been away from costly batch processing methods to more tightly controlled processes.

JIT has taught a lesson to the employees of W-L: "If you don't make things right the first time, then no amount of testing of the items in batches will make you productive." W-L now uses random sampling of items such as capsules. Previously, they inspected each one. W-L's change to JIT at 57 of their 103 plants has reaped savings of about $300 million a year, nearly 10 percent of their annual sales, without layoffs or massive investment in new technology.

As American firms seek to reduce their inventories and costs to become more competitive, they have begun to reexamine their organizational objectives. At Chevron, for example, the purchasing manager has determined that the company is "in the business of finding and processing hydrocarbons and not in the business of carrying and managing the inventories necessary to perform this function." This realization has led the firm to release the responsibility of maintaining inventory to the suppliers. Chevron now requires their suppliers to make deliveries according to Chevron's schedule [Sansing, 1984].

Everyone in the supply chain benefits by reducing inventory to the lowest possible point. As Ford introduced JIT production at its heavy-duty truck plant in Kentucky, Firestone had to switch the tire sourcing point from Mansfield to Dayton, Ohio. By combining computerized ordering and halving inventory, Firestone has been able to reduce its own finished goods inventory. In addition, its production planning is no longer guesswork [Feldman, 1984].

3-7. JIT DELIVERY AND TRANSPORTATION

As manufacturers adopt the concept of JIT in their operations, the pressure to conform has been very strong for those in delivery and transportation. JIT Delivery cannot be accomplished without JIT transportation. Several freight carriers have recognized this need and have modified their operations accordingly.

Ryder/P.I.E., headquartered in Jacksonville, Florida, is one of a handful of leading-edge trucking companies able to provide manufacturers and their suppliers with freight service designed to accommodate JIT assembly systems. Ryder delivers struts from GM's Delco Products Division in Dayton, Ohio, to the Oldsmobile plant in Lansing, Michigan, on a JIT basis.

To accommodate the request for JIT transportation from other industries also, Ryder/P.I.E. has been developing a new concept in transportation. The "repeatable process," as called by the company, involves establishing process centers in the vicinities of the assembly plants it serves. The process center acts as an extension of the assembly and manufacturing system. It is not a warehouse. As the company's customers(vendors) receive production instructions electronically from their users, it updates the inventory records at its center, processes the parts, and delivers them to the users' plants at predetermined intervals.

As JIT is introduced, the standards under which carriers must operate have been tightened. Historically, U.S. companies dealt with large shipments over long distances. Now the changes in production techniques call for frequent, small deliveries. This has led many companies to switch to truck shipments in place of rail shipments, although rail lines are responding to this trend by offering their version of JIT [Heydt, 1984].

Altered Supplier-Carrier-Buyer Relationships

All these changes have produced another new concept in the relationships between the supplier, carrier and buyer. In order to succeed, the carriers realize that they must provide more than just transportation and they have found themselves becoming partners in the customer's manufacturing and distribution process.

Some suppliers, such as Davidson Rubber in Dover, New Hampshire, expect carriers to sign transportation contracts which entail very exacting performance standards. If the delivery commitments are not met, the carriers agree to pay a penalty. Motor carriers, sensing that JIT operations are here to stay, are becoming more aggressive in their efforts to help auto distribution managers across the country meet the challenge. J.C. Penney, a retailer that places heavy emphasis on precise delivery times, has established a service-standards group in the distribution department to measure on-time performance of carriers.

The buyer-led move to keep up with the industry trend can be observed in two electronics firms also. Xerox has installed statistical process control for all their vendors who furnish parts and materials for new Xerox products. Any vendor who also needs help on quality control methods can get it directly from Xerox. Packard Electronics has devised a vendor evaluation system which, among other things, encourages supplier participation in product improvements and reducing costs.

This system generates quarterly (or monthly for substandard performance) reports on vendor performance.

3-8. QUALITY CONTROL

As we saw earlier, JIT production is not possible to achieve without total quality control. This is because a defective part disrupts the flow of production when all processes are operating with a minimal level of inventory.

Japanese quality control philosophy has been used at many manufacturing facilities in the U.S. successfully, and defect rates have decreased substantially. For example, the maker of Panasonic took over a Motorola television plant, and reduced defects from 150 per 100 sets produced to three defects per 100 sets produced over an eight-year period, using basically the same work force [Kaplan, 1983].

Changing the conventional produce-and-rework-if-defective routine to a zero-defects concept does not require heavy, new capital investment, just a total commitment from the top management down to plant workers. The mental attitude of all those involved needs to be changed. A crucial element in the implementation of total quality control is the emphasis on the coordinated group efforts toward the elimination of defects. This has led to the creation and constant utilization of quality control (QC) circles in Japan.

Many American firms are using some form of QC circles. The International Association of Quality Circles reports that its membership now includes some 2,000 American firms [Main, 1984]. A large percentage of these firms, attempting to improve product quality through worker involvement in QC circles, however, have had only limited success.

At General Motors, QC circles have been adopted and abandoned several times. Among the mistakes GM made in instituting QC circles was the failure to get the support of the union. Unions in the U.S. have seen QC circles as an invasion of their authority. As a result, according to Main [1984], the issues that a GM QC circle can address have been narrowed down to making the job easier.

Lawler and Mohrman [1985] cite the most common reasons for the limited success of QC circles as stemming from the lack of commitment of the management and employees — inadequate training, insufficient number of volunteers, inability of volunteers to learn the procedures, and lack of financial support.

3-9. MANAGEMENT-UNION RELATIONSHIP AND WORKFORCE STRATEGY

The Japanese firms have not encountered serious resistance from the unions to the introduction of various productivity-increasing measures. Japanese unions are company-based. The American firms must deal with the industry-wide unions that assume an adversarial relationship with the management. Unions are not convinced of any member benefit resulting from such changes as QC circles, reduction in labor classifications in the plant, and loosened restrictions on job specifications.

For example, when the 1985 Chrysler strike was over, it was understood that the new contract only called for a union effort to foster changes in plant-level contracts that dictate the labor classifications which, according to the lessons learned from the Japanese, should be simplified to improve manufacturing flexibility and efficiency.

Some companies have been able to work with the unions in much the same fashion as the Japanese. Recently, companies have experimented at the plant level with an entirely different workforce strategy. Companies, such as General Foods at Topeka, Kansas; Cummins in Jamestown, New York; and Proctor & Gamble in Ohio — have successfully implemented the new strategy. The results indicate that a truly committed work force can increase the productivity dramatically [Walton, 1985].

Another example of the difference a committed work force can make is found in the initial success story of the joint venture between GM and Toyota located in Fremont, California. The refurbished plant, previously owned by GM, has been hailed as a major success by union and company officials and labor experts. One year after the operations began at the plant, the cars, rolling off the assembly line there, are regarded as "very high quality" cars. The quality test revealed that the rate of "perfect" cars produced is unusually high compared to previous GM cars.

The accomplishment is noteworthy since nearly 90 percent of the hourly workers are the veteran union workers who had a reputation for militancy and absenteeism at the previous GM plant. This reflects the positive response U.S. workers have shown to management methods adopted from the Toyota system. Workers are deeply involved in quality control. They have been given the right to stop the production line without fear of discipline if they think they can not do high-quality work safely [Weinstein, 1985].

GM's Saturn plant is introducing the Japanese concept and starting some fairly radical innovation :

- The distinctions between workers and managers are blurred. For example, there will be no reserved parking, and one lunchroom for all.
- Workers will not be restricted in their tasks. Labor classifications will be limited to six — one for all unskilled workers and up to five for skilled employees.
- Production will be by work groups of six to 15 people and groups will interact. Work standards will be set jointly by labor and management representatives.
- Traditional hourly wages will be replaced by salaries. Base salary will be only 80 percent of the prevailing auto industry rate, but Saturn workers could increase their earnings significantly through bonuses tied to productivity and profits.

Although what actual benefits will be reaped through the new arrangements like one at Saturn will remain to be observed, radical departures from the traditional labor-management relationship are being made in various industries.

3-10. FURTHER CONSIDERATIONS

These changes, nevertheless, are accompanied by entrenched policies and personalities resistant to change. According to one report, manufacturing executives at Warner-Lambert first resisted the change by saying that, without weeks of inventories, they "wouldn't be able to sleep nights." A financial executive reacted differently: "While they are sleeping nights, I'm lying awake trying to figure where I'll get the money to pay for those inventories."

Problems are encountered by firms regardless of its size and industry. Even in closely-held small business, according to Williams [1985], it is often difficult to introduce new concepts to the entire organization. Various functional areas in the organization face potentially disconcerting changes in their responsibilities and operating procedures. Although the advantages of JIT and other Japanese techniques have been proven, adoption of these methods takes a careful planning and implementation.

For example, when JIT is implemented and inventories are reduced substantially in a firm which uses a LIFO inventory method, the firm may face a possibility of a sudden tax hike. As inventories decrease, the understated, basic LIFO layer is dipped into. This causes the cost of goods sold to be understated, and the resulting increase in taxable income may make the firm subject to a heavy tax levy. Accordingly, tax planning is needed before a firm makes a change to JIT.[8] This will require the accounting area to maintain a close coordination with the production, purchasing, and other areas within the firm.

3-11. SUMMARY

In this chapter, we observed new management practices which had been developed by overseas manufacturers and had been used successfully, leading to their superior competitive position in world markets. U.S. industry, nevertheless, is responding to the challenges from overseas by introducing the new techniques into their operations.

Further, some U.S. corporations such as General Motors have successfully implemented an innovative production management technique, called Optimized Production Technology (OPT), which is a software system developed in the U.S. The system has proven to be a big success in reducing inventory. Details of OPT are presented in the appendix to Chapter 4.

In the next chapter, we will look at various aspects of the factory of the future, the present state of CIM, and how U.S. industry is responding to the new challenges in technology.

REFERENCES

Cope, R.E., "Japanese Productivity: Can It Work Here?" *Modern Casting* (October 1982), pp.22-25.

Feldman, J., "Transportation Changes — Just in Time," *Handling and Shipping Management* (September 1984), pp.46-50.

Fisher, A.B., "Behind the Hype at GM's Saturn," *Fortune* (November 11, 1985), pp. 34-49.

Forbes, "Codes for Carmakers" (December 31, 1984), pp.12-13.

Hatvany, N. and V. Pucik, "An Integrated Management System: Lessons from the Japanese Experience," *Academy of Management Review* (July 1981), pp. 469-478.

Heydt, B., "Made in Japan," *Chiltons Distribution* (April 1984), pp.50-55.

Industry Week, "Can Kanban Ban Inventory Blues?" (July 26, 1982), pp.21-22.

---

[8] In order to avoid the one-time, high tax levy, a firm may consider switching to a FIFO inventory method prior to the conversion to JIT. This is just one of many options that are available.

Kaplan, R.S., "Measuring Manufacturing Performance: A New Challenge for Managerial Accounting Research," *The Accounting Review* (October 1983), pp.686-705.

Kimura, O. and H. Terada, "Design and Analysis of Pull System — A Method of Multi-Stage Production Control," *International Journal of Production Research* (May-June 1981), pp.241-253.

Lawler, E.E. and S.A. Mohrman, "Quality Circles after the Fad," *Harvard Business Review* (January-February 1985), pp.65-71.

Main, J., "The Trouble with Managing Japanese-Style," *Fortune* (April 12, 1984), pp.50-56.

McGovern, T., "Why Japan's Management Style May Not Fit Here," *Nation's Business* (August 1983), pp.30-31.

Monden, Y., *Toyota Production System* (Atlanta: Institute of Industrial Engineers, 1983).

Murrin, T., "Rejecting the Traditional Ways of Doing Business" (Chicago: American Production and Inventory Control Society, October 1982).

Newsweek, "An Ardent Suitor for Saturn" (January 21, 1985), pp. 56-57.

Newsweek, "Chrysler Takes a U-Turn" (October 28, 1985), p.62.

Ouchi, W., "Organizational Paradigms: A Commentary on Japanese Management and Theory Z Organizations," *Organizational Dynamics* (Spring 1981), pp. 36-43.

Ouchi, W. and A.M. Jaeger, "Type Z Organization: Stability in the Midst of Mobility," *Academy of Management Review* (April 1978), pp. 305-314.

Ouchi, W. and J.B. Johnson, "Types of Organizational Control and Their Relationship to Emotional Well-Being," *Administrative Science Quarterly* (Spring 1978), pp.293-317.

Ouchi, W. and R.L. Price, "Hierarchies, Clans, and Theory Z: A New Perspective on Organization Development," *Organizational Dynamics* (Autumn 1978), pp. 24-44.

Sansing, B., "Chevron Idea Could Help Supply Firms," *Tulsa Business Chronicle* (October 22, 1984), pp.1-5.

Schonberger, R.J. and A. Ansari, "'Just-in-time' Purchasing Can Improve Quality," *Journal of Purchasing and Materials Management* (Spring 1984), pp. 2-6.

Sugimori, Y., K. Kusunoki, F. Cho, and S. Uchikawa, "Toyota Production System and Kanban System - Materialization of Just-in-Time and Respect-for-Human System," *International Journal of Production Research* (November 1977), pp. 553-564.

Walton, R.E., "From Control to Commitment in the Workplace," *Harvard Business Review* (March-April 1985), pp.77-84.

Weinstein, H., "U.S. Car Workers Adapt to Japanese Style," *The Los Angeles Times* (December 22, 1985), pp. 1, 16, and 17.

Williams, J., "Just-in-Time Ideally Suited to Smaller Manufacturing Operations," *The CPA Journal* (March 1985), pp. 81-83.

SUGGESTED ADDITIONAL READINGS

Business Week, "Fighting Back: It Can Work" (August 26, 1985), pp.62-68.

Harbour, J., "Just in Time, Not Just in Case," *Corporate Accounting* (Spring 1985), pp. 5-8.

Hayes, R.H., "Why Japanese Factories Work," *Harvard Business Review* (July-August 1981), pp. 57-66.

King, B., L. Krajewski, and L. Ritaman, "Manufacturing Performance — Pulling the Right Levers," *Harvard Business Review* (March-April 1984), pp.143-152.

Manuel, W.G., "Productivity Experiences at Nucor," in Buehler and Shetty, *Productivity Improvement:Case Studies of Proven Practice* (New York: AMACOM, 1981), Chapter 4.

Ouchi, W.G., *Theory Z: How American Business Can Meet the Japanese Challenge* (Menlo Park, CA: Addison-Wesley,1981).

Walleigh, R.C., "What's Your Excuse for Not Using JIT?" *Harvard Business Review* (March-April 1986), pp. 38-54.

CHAPTER FOUR

Changing Technology and Its Impact on U.S. Industry

4-1. THE FACTORY OF THE FUTURE

In Chapter One there was a brief discussion of changing technology and its impact on U.S. industry. In this chapter the entire issue of changing technology and its effects on U.S. industry will be examined in more detail.

For decades manufacturers have tried to replace their human workforce with machines in an attempt to reduce labor costs. As early as the 1960s, many manufacturers wanted to introduce robots for that purpose. In the new era of automation, however, the purpose is not merely to achieve labor cost savings, but also to attain more flexibility in the manufacturing process.

Confronted with the formidable challenges from overseas competition, U.S. firms must find ways to respond to changing market conditions quickly, tailor products to different consumer tastes, introduce new and innovative products, and accomplish all these at reduced costs. Previously, mass production was the primary means of cost savings. In a fully automated factory, however, the firm can "make the first copy of a product for little more than the cost of the thousandth." Accordingly, firms "optimized for economies of scale may become obsolete" [Business Week, 1986].

33

Most industry leaders agree that the ultimate solution to the problem U.S. industry faces in its competition with foreign companies can be found in computer-integrated manufacturing (CIM). With CIM, a firm is able to link all of the functions of its offices and factories through total automation using computers. As a result, the firm will be able to manufacture one-of-a-kind products in small batches for specific customers on short notice. The automated manufacturing systems will replace the mass production of often-defective, standard items with a job-shop production of almost-perfect, unique items.

The competitive strength of U.S. industry will certainly increase with CIM, and since the processing time will be greatly reduced, firms will no longer need large inventories of finished products. Firms can produce to the order. In addition, CIM has the potential to make labor costs a negligible portion of total production costs. Accordingly, the winners in the new markets will be those firms that can respond to changing consumer tastes more quickly with new, better products at quicker turnarounds, rather than those with lower labor costs. U.S. firms, as they are located closer to the consumer market and have better access to computer technology, are in a superior competitive position in the new era compared to their foreign counterparts.

In the following sections, we will look at various aspects of the factory of the future, the present state of CIM, and how U.S. industry is responding to the new challenges in technology.

4-2. CAD, CAE, AND CAM

An automated factory should be capable of performing various functions with the aid of computers including product design, engineering, and manufacturing, as well as other management systems. The factory could first allow product designers to optimize their ideas on new products using a computer-aided design (CAD) system. Designers can move pieces of design around their drawings, manipulate them to see how the shapes change from various angles, and so forth, on their CAD terminals. As computer technology develops, CAD systems are made more convenient and economical. The kind of CAD systems that once required mainframe computers now run on microcomputer networks. And the benefits of CAD can be quite significant: At Chrysler, a network of over 500 design workstations have reduced the time it takes to generate engineering drawings from three months 30 years ago to 15 minutes today [The Economist, 1986].

In the factory of the future, product designers will work on computer terminals, which are linked to central databases and softwares, to find out whether a new product will be feasible to produce with the available machines and how much the cost will be. This is done by sending the CAD information through a computer-aided engineering (CAE) system. Presently, they need help from production engineers to answer those questions.

Once the CAE systems verify the feasibility of a new product design, the necessary information for manufacturing the product can be transmitted to a computer-aided manufacturing (CAM) system. There will be very little time lag between design and manufacturing. The factory will no longer need to rearrange machines with new sets of tools to prepare for the production of a new product. The job will be done by a small number of versatile machining centers. The CAM system would dispatch production orders to electronic machine tools, robots, and other automated work stations.

4-3. FLEXIBLE MANUFACTURING SYSTEMS (FMS)

CAD and CAE systems can speed up designing and testing processes. Today's factories, nevertheless, contain only isolated islands of automation. Various work stations must be linked by human "bridges" that cause delays. That is why the dream of CIM seems so attractive: A fully automated factory that does not need human bridges. CIM, however, is yet to materialize.

In the meantime, a scaled-down version of CIM has become popular in manufacturing. It is known as flexible manufacturing systems (FMS). An FMS is a bundle of machines that can be reprogrammed to switch from one production run to another. It consists of a cluster of machine tools and a system of conveyor belts that shuttle the workpiece from tool to tool. FMS are compared very favorably to the transfer line used in mass production. Transfer lines move workpieces in a fixed order past a sequence of machine tools. Therefore, the benefits of FMS lie in the flexibility to change from making one product to making another [The Economist, 1986].

An FMS employs robots and computer-controlled material handling systems to link various standalone, computer-programmed machine tools (called numerical control machines). A system-level computer controller is also used to coordinate the manufacturing system. The major strength of an FMS is its ability to produce a "family of products," compared to only a narrow range of products. For example, a General Electric plant in Erie, Pennsylvania, is capable of producing diesel engines of substantially different sizes on the same automated production line, without substantial retooling and setups [Dilts and Russell, 1985].

More specifically, according to Dilts and Russell [p. 36], FMS provides the following benefits:

1. More variety of products as compared to conventional automation without the low rate of capacity utilization of a typical job shop system.
2. Better product quality thanks to accuracy and repeatability of the production process.
3. Shorter machine setup times for a new production run, which results in reduced lead times to meet customer demands. This, in turn, decreases work-in-process inventories, and, subsequently, plant space.
4. Reduced direct labor costs, and capital costs of human environmental protection.
5. Stability in production even with machine breakdown, because of computer scheduling, which also allows instant responses to changes in demand.

While FMS produces these benefits, the implementation of it requires careful planning and preparation to avoid some pitfalls. First, a firm contemplating an adoption of FMS needs to plan for an almost certain resistance from employees who fear the possible loss of their jobs. Second, the firm must come up with an innovative approach to justifying the capital investment, since the conventional capital budgeting techniques may not yield positive results. (This issue will be further discussed in Chapter Five.) Last, there may be a lack of qualified engineers and other management systems to support FMS.

Since it is necessary to coordinate the computerized manufacturing system with other management systems to link related functions, CAD/CAM should be supported by Manufacturing Resource Planning, an information system model of the total manufacturing environment. We will look at Manufacturing Resource Planning in the next section.

4-4. MANUFACTURING RESOURCE PLANNING (MRP II)

In an automated manufacturing environment, it is essential to develop and maintain a common data base for various functional units, such as purchasing, engineering, personnel, finance, marketing, as well as production. All these units need to have access to the same information to keep proper control over resources for optimum results.

Manufacturing Resource Planning, called MRP II, serves this purpose well. It provides a vital link between two classes of managerial activities: strategic planning and management control (in the area of manufacturing). Through the use of MRP II managers can simulate and compare competing strategies in light of actual manufacturing capacities and changing environments. Figure 4.1 illustrates a process of MRP II.

The process of MRP II starts with product demand forecast supplied by the marketing area and approved by management. Based on the forecast by time period,

Figure 4.1. The Process of Manufacturing Resource Planning.

a manufacturing plan is adopted with other inputs from the various functional areas such as purchasing, production, accounting, and so forth.

In the adopted manufacturing plan, some adjustments are made to accommodate changing demand: Adjust production rate, inventory levels of finished goods and work in process, and/or the size of work force. For the evaluation and simulation of these adjustments, individually or collectively, MRP II can be used. The outcome will be a selected manufacturing plan that leads to the optimum utilization of the firm's resources.

The manufacturing plan, stated usually in physical units, now becomes a common data base, since the unit data can be translated into standard hours and dollar amounts for all related departments' business plans. These pave the way for the preparation of the master production schedule.

The master production schedule, prepared semiannually or annually, includes production schedules for finished goods, parts, and subassemblies usually on a weekly basis. Various factors such as production capacity, materials and parts requirements, and other production details of the plant are incorporated into the master production schedule.

Once the master production schedule is prepared and approved, it should be translated into material requirements for each time period, as well as the periodic needs for components and subassemblies. This represents an enormous amount of calculation and clerical work, which should be done by computers. A set of logically linked rules, decision processes, and records used for the translation is called material requirements planning (MRP).

As illustrated in Figure 4.1, MRP receives its information input primarily from the master production schedule. Other inputs are also received from an inventory file, a product structure file containing data on the need to purchase or produce various components, and a production routing file that explains the work sequence, production lead time, lot size, etc. for all products.

Based on these data, the mainframe computer will determine material requirements for each component in each time period needed to produce items in the master production schedule, adjusted for the inventory on hand and in transit. Then the system can plan in advance a series of released production orders or purchase orders, since the information is already available on when items are needed and how long it takes to get them.

As the material requirements are determined, the needs for machine and human capacities can also be planned for the same time period. If the necessary capacity is not available, the master production schedule can be revised as the system has the feedback capability to monitor and update itself at the right time.

MRP II, when successfully employed, provides a common data base for different functional units in the firm, such as manufacturing, purchasing, finance, etc. The fully automated factory, however, needs to have the capability to combine all the computer-run activities discussed so far for the factory. Knowledge on how the factory should operate - that exists in the heads of operations experts and planners - must be captured in some way to integrate the above mentioned activities for a firm. Expert systems, discussed in the next section, is the answer to that question.

4-5. EXPERT SYSTEMS

Expert systems are computer programs that can integrate databases with rules of thumb extracted from reasoning and decision-making processes of human experts. Accordingly, unlike conventional programs, expert systems can deal with qualitative as well as quantitative data.

The following is the typical organization of expert systems:

1. Knowledge database - The rules of thumb on how the elements of a subject behave are stored in the knowledge database.
2. Domain database - The facts of a subject to be studied are stored in the domain database.
3. Database management system - This system manages the databases for the entire expert system.
4. User interface - The user of the system enters facts of a subject and addresses questions through the program called user interface.
5. Knowledge acquisition facility - The human expert's knowledge is extracted by the system through dialogue using the program called knowledge acquisition facility.
6. Inference engine - Reasoning and decision making are done by the program called inference engine.

Using the above organization and logic, expert systems, in a sense, serve as electronic consultants. They can analyze operations, answer questions, and even describe the process used to reach a conclusion [Akers, Porter, Blocher, and Mister, 1986].

4-6. CIM - THE IDEAL AND PRESENT STATE

When the previously discussed technologies are integrated into a network of total automation, as illustrated in Figure 4.2, the following will be possible:

- A firm can allow product designers to optimize their ideas on new products using a CAD system.
- The CAD information is sent through a CAE system to determine whether a new product will be feasible to produce with the available machines and to obtain a cost estimate.
- The necessary information for manufacturing the product is transmitted to a CAM system which will dispatch production orders to electronic machine tools, robots, and other automated work stations.
- MRP II is used as an information system model to coordinate computerized manufacturing with other management systems.
- Expert systems with artificial intelligence integrate computer databases with extracted rules to perform reasoning and decision making activities.

When CIM is fully implemented, a firm will not require human bridges to link isolated work stations. The manufacturer's production process will be controlled entirely through a computer network. The network can even link with the systems of suppliers and customers allowing linkage, for example, of an automaker with its parts suppliers and dealers. When dealers type customers' orders into the terminals

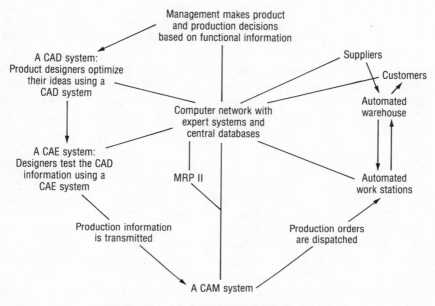

Figure 4.2. How Computer-Integrated Manufacturing Works

in their showrooms, the CIM network will place orders for parts, arrange parts shipments with suppliers, and dispatch production orders to the factory floor.

Although the dream of CIM seems so attractive, it has not yet materialized. According to Business Week, the factories of only about two dozen U.S. firms "even come close to the goal of total automation" [1986, p.73]. The slow progress toward the sure-to-come CIM is due to technological difficulty, lack of trained personnel, high cost, and management's risk-avoidance attitude.

Among the three major types of manufacturing operations - flow production of chemicals and oils on a continuous basis, mass production of discrete products, and batch production of discrete products - the last category is considered to benefit the most from automation [Gerwin, 1982]. Accordingly, tens of manufacturers with batch production process have installed FMS: the scaled-down version of CIM, which is operational at the present time.

There are slight differences between the figures reported by various sources, but there are approximately 40 FMSs in place in the U.S., with about 50 in Japan and a little higher number in Europe. The numbers are expected to grow to three or four hundred by 1990. Currently the U.S. has a technological edge, but overseas rivals are closing the gap [Business Week, 1986]. Since "Japanese manufacturers tend to go for any kind of technological innovation" [Fortune, 1986, p.94], the future race toward automation should be hotly contested.

4-7. U.S. INDUSTRY AND MANUFACTURING DEVELOPMENT

Then, how is U.S. industry really coping with the monumental task of manufacturing development? Many studies have so far reported on the subject. Most of them, however, have dealt with the subject without using any descriptive framework to explain the industry's response to technological advances. In this section, we will observe the developments through a prism of a descriptive framework provided by Wheelwright and Hayes [1984, hereinafter W & H].

There are four different types of roles that manufacturing can play in a firm's efforts to achieve overall strategic goals, according to W & H. These generic kinds of roles are viewed as indicators of the stages of a firm's development. The identified roles are used here to characterize the status of the manufacturing function in various industries.

Stage 1 - In this stage, top management regards the manufacturing function as incapable of influencing competitive success. They tend to regard manufacturing as a low-tech operation that can be run by low-skilled workers and managers. Accordingly, they try to minimize their involvement with manufacturing, and concern themselves primarily with major investment decisions based on the capital budgeting process.

Based on this view, the top managers of such firms agree to add capacity only when the need becomes obvious. They prefer to build large general-purpose facilities employing safe technologies purchased from outside vendors. W & H classify consumer products and service companies in this category. Because of the limited view, those managers find it difficult to upgrade their labor-intensive, low-tech processes when new-generation- technology products appear. Their general-purpose facilities can not compete with the highly specialized plants of world-class rivals.

Stage 2 - These companies seek to avoid major, discontinuous changes in production. Stage 2 companies treat new capital investments as the most effective means for gaining temporary competitive advantage, and view economies of scale as the most crucial type of production efficiency. Companies in auto, steel, and heavy-equipment industries are classified by W & H into this category.

These industries have an oligopolistic market structure in which existing, stable competitors want to maintain the status quo. Many companies in electronic instrument assembly and pharmaceutical production also belong in this category. Here production is considered to be fairly standardized and unsophisticated. Top managers of these companies undertake manufacturing investments only when manufacturing weaknesses have become obvious. These investments are primarily reactionary and cost-cutting in nature.

Stage 3 - The companies in this stage expect manufacturing to make a significant contribution toward strengthening their competitive position. Their investments and systems changes in production are consistent over time in the sense that long-term organizational needs are considered. They want manufacturing to be creative and managed with a long-term view, which is expressed by the adoption of one or two of the new techniques - JIT, CAD/ CAM, or robots - while continuing to run manufacturing as a Stage 2 activity.

The beer industry is classified by W & H as being in Stage 3. In the 1970s many beer companies built new, large-scale facilities and rationalized their existing operations, but didn't continue the positive strategies afterwards. When Stage 2 companies introduce new technologies in manufacturing, they do it to keep up with their industry, but not before the implications of new technologies become fully apparent.

Stage 4 - This most progressive stage of manufacturing development characterizes those companies which derive a considerable portion of competitive strategy from their manufacturing capability. In this stage, the role of manufacturing is to make a significant contribution to the competitive success of the company. Such an important role is given to manufacturing because in some industries, turning out new, superior products using the most up-to-date processes is the only way to maintain a competitive advantage.

Stage 4 companies can recognize the potential of new manufacturing technologies and try to gain expertise in them long before their implications are fully apparent, W & H state. The leading companies in so-called process-intensive industries belong in this category. In these companies, manufacturing is actively involved in the capital budgeting process by providing additional qualitative analysis to compensate for shortcomings in financial data.

The Difficult, But Crucial Decision

In Chapter Two, we looked at U.S. managers' behavior and their attitude toward innovative but risky decisions involving long-term implications. Based on the analysis made there and the nature of the companies in the first three stages discussed above, we can understand why the vast majority of U.S. manufacturers are dragging their feet in the computerization of manufacturing: Companies in Stages 1 and 2 are very much removed from the decision involving manufacturing computerization. Those in Stage 3 may make one bold move by adopting one of the new techniques such as robotics, JIT, and the like, but usually this occurs very late.

The biggest hurdle to the computerization is the difficulty of justifying the huge amount of investment the task requires. Even the scaled-down version (FMS) costs $6-7 million and the conventional technique of capital budgeting, where future cash inflows come mainly from savings in labor costs, does not provide the management with enough impetus for the change. Other reasons are the lack of qualified personnel, and still less-than-complete technology.

The fundamental reason for the slow progress, nevertheless, is U.S. managers' attitude of risk aversion, which was analyzed in Chapter Two. Those future strengths that will come from computerization - product quality improvement, increased flexibility, etc. - are not visible to the managers, and managers as a breed tend to avoid radical changes.

4-8. SUMMARY

In this chapter, the various aspects of the new technologies involved in the factory of the future, the ideal and present states of computerized manufacturing, and U.S. industry's response to the new challenge were examined. Management accountants need to be familiar with the changes taking place in the industry now and those that are forthcoming in the future, so as to fulfill the duties of designing and maintaining the information systems necessary to provide information useful for managerial decision making.

Changes that are being made are not entirely based on only technological developments. Some have originated from a completely new way of understanding how today's factories should work. Techniques such as Optimized Production Technology (OPT) are good examples. (See the Appendix at the end of this chapter for more details on OPT.) As the environment of managerial accounting changes dramatically, so should the way management accountants think. This harsh reality will form the basis of discussion in Chapter 5.

APPENDIX

Optimized Production Technology (OPT)

An American Answer

Suppose there are ten workers operating on an assembly line. The first nine workers are working at the maximum possible efficiency while the tenth worker is experiencing a problem that holds up the line. Can we say the plant as a whole is experiencing high productivity since 90 percent of our work force operates efficiently?

The answer is a definite no. In a manufacturing operation that involves work done in a sequence, a plant can work only at the pace of its slowest production process along the line. This is the main idea of OPT. Bottlenecks hold up the entire production line. If a factory's work is simulated accurately prior to the actual run, bottlenecks along the production process can be spotted in advance. OPT is a software system written for the simulation by E. Goldratt.

OPT is designed to eliminate excess inventory much like JIT. From the above example, it becomes obvious that the parts the first nine workers produced at their maximum efficiency will be piled up since the tenth worker can not process them. If there is a bottleneck down the line, why waste materials by processing them even using robots and leaving them idle at a high cost? OPT is an American response to the Japanese challenge in manufacturing.

Rules of OPT

First, production managers are advised to focus on maintaining a smooth flow of materials. OPT makes it clear that the maximum utilization of workers and materials should not be stressed more than the smooth flow of materials, especially in assembly line and process-intensive operations. OPT emphasizes throughput - how much a production system produces to generate money through sales - more than the efficiency of individual workers.

Under OPT, a manufacturing plant is advised to balance flow, not plant capacity, to increase profit. The reason is explained using two phenomena of manufacturing: dependent events and statistical fluctuations. Most manufacturing operations are performed in a sequential manner involving dependent events, while manufacturing data such as sales estimates, production rates, spoilage rates, available work force, etc. are subject to statistical fluctuations.

The undesirable nature of balancing capacity can be illustrated by the "rolling die" example of Fox,* which is summarized below.

Assume there are six sequential manufacturing operations all of which have the same average capacity of 3.5 units a day calculated as follows:

$$\text{Average capacity} = (1 + 2 + 3 + 4 + 5 + 6 \text{ units}) / 6$$
$$= 3.5 \text{ units}$$

Although the actual production rate fluctuates statistically from 1 to 6 units a day, the plant's average output per month (20 days) appears to be 70 units. (3.5 units a day x 20 days.) Is this assumption valid in a real world situation?

Fox's simulation to test the validity works as follows:

1. Start with 7 units of buffer inventory, which represents two days average usage, as the amount of inventory between each of the operations.
2. Roll a die. The number you get on each roll is the day's potential production and should average around 3.5 units if a reasonable number of trials is allowed.
3. Actual production should be less than or equal to the number obtained above. For example, suppose your number on the die is 4 and only 2 units of inventory are available for production. This happens sooner or later in reality.. Then the actual production for the day is 2 units because of the inventory constraint.

Due to statistical fluctuations, your plant will experience excesses and shortages in inventory. Therefore, the average production of the plant will be less than the 70 units projected previously. In the meantime, inventory levels will keep going up resulting in extra costs for the plant. The simulation demonstrates the pitfalls in balancing capacity.

Another Look at EOQ

OPT makes production managers take another look at the economic order quantity (EOQ) model and the MRP system. When the EOQ model is applied to production, it is supposed to provide a single lot size that leads to the minimization of cost. Under the rules of OPT, this theory is disputed. Citing the real-world experience of seasoned professionals, Goldratt proposes to treat the batch size as variable, not as fixed. Plants are advised not to run the same-size batch for each operation.

This supposedly corrects the technical flaw in EOQ which has been found to be unrealistic in practice. According to OPT, various numbers of parts pass through different machines, and the plant needs to vary the lot size to maintain the smooth flow of materials in all operations.

A New Way of Thinking

The gist of OPT is to increase profit by boosting throughput, while keeping inventory and operating expenses low. Bottlenecks are spotted, controlled, and

---

*The article, "Main Bottleneck on the Factory Floor?" by R. E. Fox, published in *Management Review* (November 1984), pp.55-61, describes OPT in reasonable detail for business readers.

used to maintain the smooth flow of materials and parts through the system. Labor and machine hours are scheduled accordingly.

Since OPT uses various ideas that may look radically different from the conventional viewpoint, managers in the factory and in the corporate headquarters need to think differently in order to implement OPT successfully. OPT is an innovative production technology, like JIT, that looks very promising to U.S. industry. Corporate giants such as General Motors and General Electric have already adopted OPT in their operations.

REFERENCES

Akers, M.D., G.L. Porter, E.J. Blocher, and W.G. Mister, "Expert Systems for Management Accountants," *Management Accounting* (March 1986), pp. 30-34.

Business Week, "How Automation Could Save the Day" (March 3, 1986), pp. 72-74.

Dilts, D.M. and G.W. Russell, "Accounting for the Factory of the Future," *Management Accounting* (April 1985), pp. 34-40.

The Economist, "The Factory of the Future" (April 5, 1986), pp. 97-99.

Fortune, "Networking: Japan's Latest Computer Craze" (July 7, 1986), pp. 94-96.

Fox, R.E., "Main Bottleneck on the Factory Floor?" *Management Review* (November 1984), pp. 55-61.

Gerwin, D., "Do's and Don'ts of Computerized Manufacturing," *Harvard Business Review* (March-April 1982), pp.107-116.

Wheelwright, S.C. and R.H. Hayes, "Competing through Manufacturing," *Harvard Business Review* (January-February 1985), pp.99-103.

OTHER SUGGESTED READINGS

Anderson, J.C., R.G. Schroeder, S.E. Tupy, and E.M. White, *Materials Requirements Planning: A Study of Implementation and Practice* (American Production and Inventory Control Society, 1981).

Blackburn, J.D., D.H. Kropp, and R.A. Millen, "A Comparison of Strategies to Dampen Nervousness in MRP Systems," *Management Science* (April 1986), pp. 413-429.

Daniels, S.K., "MRP Systems Are Not All Alike," *Production and Inventory Management* (First Quarter 1986), pp. 47-51.

Gallimore, J.M., "Planning to Automate Your Factory," *Production Engineering* (May 1983), pp. 50-52.

Gullo, K., "Factory Automation: Closing the Gap," *Datamation* (October 15, 1985), pp.46-50.

Hegland, D.E., "CIM — The Foundation for Factory Automation," *Production Engineering* (May 1985), pp. 36-42.

Huber, R.F., "Justification: Barrier to Competitive Manufacturing," *Production* (September 1985), pp. 46-51.

Jain, A.K., "Education for Factory Automation," *Manufacturing Systems* (September 1985), pp. 50-51.

Miller, J.G. and T.E. Vollman, "The Hidden Factory," *Harvard Business Review* (September-October 1985), pp.142-150.

Production, "CIM Must Start at the Top" (March 1985), pp.43-49.

Rosenthal, S.R., "Progress Toward the 'Factory of the Future'," *Journal of Operations Management* (May 1984), pp. 203-229.

Safizadeh, M.H. and F. Raafat, "Formal/Informal Systems and MRP Implementation," *Production and Inventory Management* (First Quarter 1986), pp. 115-121.

Stavro, B., "Strategic Withdrawal," *Forbes* (February 10, 1986), pp.34-35.

Stein, E.S., "MRP II and the Management of Change," *Manufacturing Systems* (May 1986), pp. 47-48.

CHAPTER FIVE

The Influences of the Changing Environment on Product Costing Systems and Control

5-1. A PARADIGM SHIFT NEEDED?

Every field of science, according to Kuhn [1962], has a normal paradigm that is thought of as the culture that defines the areas of research, the methods of inquiry, and the standards of what constitutes the research progress. Over time, every normal paradigm gets depleted, and a period of relatively little discovery follows.

If the scholars in that field can adopt a fundamentally different conception of their paradigm through a major paradigm shift, Kuhn argues, then their field may find itself propelled into a period of creativity and of progress. A paradigm shift takes place when the normal paradigm cannot explain new events.

Faced with the fundamental changes in the environment taking place, management accountants may need a new paradigm within which to map the proper courses of action. The actions are called for since the major objective of the managerial accounting function within an organization is to design and maintain control systems that facilitate planning for the implementation of strategies and motivate managers to achieve the organizational goals [Anthony, Dearden, and Bedford, 1984].

The task of management accountants in this aspect is a formidable one. While the production function can introduce robots and other computerized manufacturing technologies into their work as soon as the cost is justified, or top management acquires faith in it, the managerial accounting function must make all other functions within the organization understand and accept any new control system they devise, before the new system can become operational.

In the area of product costing systems and control, the traditional cost accounting model assumes an environment of the mass production of a few standardized items. When the environment undergoes fundamental changes which permit efficient production of small batches of customized products on short notice, for example, a new setting for cost systems and control is introduced [Kaplan, 1984].

Many authors have already proposed and discussed what needs to be done in the changing environment which is already here or forthcoming soon. Their ideas and suggested solutions, which will be discussed in this and the following chapters, serve as useful guides for management accountants.

There exists, nevertheless, a question of whether these piecemeal approaches would provide a coherent set of answers needed to guide management accountants in the coming decade. Should the entire structure and underlying concepts of management accounting change to accommodate new needs in the new era? Do we really need a new paradigm in this field?

Several published studies shed some light on this by suggesting some new directions management accounting research can take in the future. There needs to be, however, continued and well-integrated efforts made by practitioners and academicians to find a comprehensive conceptual framework that can be used for different systems and functions.[1]

In this chapter, we will study the influences of the changing environment on product costing systems and control. The influences on management control and performance measurement will be discussed in Chapter Six. Special topics will be covered in Chapter Seven.

5-2. METHODS OF MANUFACTURE AND STAGES OF THE CHANGES

As a preparation for subsequent discussions, we can look at the methods of manufacture and the stages of the changes in general. The forces of change — which include advances in manufacturing technology, easier but different cost collection processes, and change in cost structure, among others — work differently depending on what methods of manufacture are used.

Before we discuss the effects of the changes, therefore, we need to understand methods of manufacture first.

Methods of Manufacture

Three primary methods of manufacture are found in the manufacturing industry [Gerwin, 1982]:

1. Flow production of gases and liquids.
2. Mass production of discrete parts.
3. Batch production of discrete parts.

---

[1] The National Association of Accountants has led the efforts to deal with the challenges of technological change by organizing the nation's first conference on the issue. The conference, titled "Cost Accounting for the 90s," was held in Boston, Massachusetts, on April 28-29, 1986. Over 250 accountants from industry, government, and academia attended it.

Categories 1 and 2 relate to large-volume single products or a few standardized products which Kaplan referred to in the above section. They involve continuous operations which follow a cost-efficient, predetermined sequence. Those operations require specialized equipment and are heavily automated, according to Gerwin.

Category 3, which represents more than 35 percent of the U.S. manufacturing base, involves manufacture of various different products of low volume and low standardization. The production process is intermittent, follows no invariable sequence, and requires general-purpose equipment. In this mode, product units remain in process for substantially longer intervals, and have higher unit costs. The operations are less automated compared to the first two categories.

Changes and their Stages

A pull system, the essence of JIT, can operate most efficiently in a repetitive manufacturing environment, where schedules are sufficiently level so that the manufacturing processes can react to the pull signals. Striving to reduce inventory will yield desirable results only when such efforts expose process deficiencies that lead to process improvements [Sauers, 1986].

In a JIT environment, where a pull system functions, MRP is still useful for long-run production and capacity planning, purchasing requirements planning, and coordinating activities if the company is large, has multiple plants, and produces multiple products. This is because, in such an environment, there are many transactions, information, and decision making which call for a disciplined and controlled setting. MRP is regarded as a building block for JIT [Johansson, 1986].

How, then, do the changes discussed in previous chapters take place? Or, more precisely, how should the changes be planned? The changes, Hronec contends, should be made according to the proper sequence of stages which are:

Stage 1. Simplify the process first. Introducing JIT or OPT is one example.

Stage 2. Install some islands of automation.

Stage 3. Integrate those islands through a data network, which means the implementation of CIM [1986].

Following the order, according to Hronec, is very important. Some U.S. manufacturers automated (Stage 2) before simplifying their processes (Stage 1) which resulted in a substantial waste of time, money and efforts. For example, automatic storage and retrieval systems they had installed prior to JIT became unnecessary after JIT manufacturing was implemented because there was no longer any significant amount of inventory to deal with.

JIT, accordingly, is considered to be a prerequisite for automation. Some companies yank out robots and other flexible manufacturing processes because the process redesign has led them to realize that the automated part is not needed in a JIT environment [Johansson, 1986].

Is CIM, the ultimate stage of computer manufacturing technology, for every industry? According to Johansson, it is not. Automotive, aerospace, and electronics industries are best suited for CIM and have partially implemented it. Other industries must carefully evaluate their needs before making the commitment, since about 80 percent of all benefits from CIM can be derived from JIT manufacturing [Hronec, 1986].

5-3. SOME EARLY EFFECTS OF THE CHANGES OBSERVED

When Hewlett-Packard (H-P) introduced JIT and total quality control (TQC) at its new printed circuit fabrication facility in 1983, fundamental changes in the product costing system took place. Traditional costing methods did not suit the changed manufacturing environment, and "information flows between the accounting, production, and material functions were radically altered."

According to Hunt, Garrett, and Merz (HG & M) [1985], the changes in manufacturing made the accounting systems much simpler at H-P. One example cited is that about 100,000 journal entries per month were eliminated due to the simplified accounting for work-in-process inventories.

Job Order Costing

Accountants' Cost Handbook states that the major objective of a job order cost system is to charge correctly the three cost elements of direct material, direct labor, and manufacturing overhead to the individual job orders. These job orders are not usually alike, nor do they pass through the same manufacturing processes. Therefore, cost information should be accumulated for each job [Dickey, 1960, section 11].

While this distinctive feature of job order costing should still be a reality in those industries such as construction, heavy machinery production, shipbuilding, etc., substantial changes in product costing have taken place in other industries. For example, when a medical products company implemented JIT and total quality control methods in its operations, costs did not need to be accumulated by individual job nor by individual work station. The costs could be accumulated at the department level for each period. Previously, the product cost accumulation for all production in the entire plant was done through job orders [Seglund and Ibarreche, 1984].

In a flexible manufacturing environment described in previous chapters, workers (and even materials) are frequently transferred between job orders to insure a smooth flow of process. This will certainly disrupt the accounting department's attempt to trace the costs of three elements to different job orders.

Job orders, the primary scheduling and cost-tracking tool in a traditional environment, also become less useful in the new setting, when lot sizes become too small to have a unique job order attached to each lot [Wright, 1986]. It is, however, ironic to hear HG & M's report that line managers and production workers at the H-P plant, have been able to understand production reports a lot better since the cost accountants discontinued tracking direct labor costs and factory overhead costs [p.61].

As the levels of work-in-process and finished goods inventory are reduced substantially, in some successful cases — like H-P — to insignificant levels, cost accountants have begun not to charge direct labor and factory overhead costs to work-in-process and finished goods accounts. Instead, they charge them to the cost of goods sold directly. The substantial reduction in accounting costs has overridden the marginal decrease in the accuracy of the calculated costs for these firms.

Process Costing

Process cost systems, unlike job order cost systems, emphasize an evaluation of a process or department by looking at the total number of units produced in a certain period [Dopuch, Birnberg, and Demski, 1974, p.525]. The total manufacturing costs are divided by the total units produced to obtain a unit cost. The resultant unit cost is then used to calculate the costs of inventories in process and goods completed. The units of output in process costing, however, are not expressed in terms of equivalent units. Equivalent units indicates the amount of work done.

A typical calculation of equivalent units takes the following format:

	Materials	Conversion
(1) Units completed	xxx	xxx
(2) Plus ending work in process	xxx(% assigned)	xxx(% assigned)
(3) Equals amount of work done to date	xxx	xxx
(4) (Less)Beginning work in process	(xxx)(% assigned)	(xxx)(% assigned)
(5) Equals amount of work done in the current period	xxx	xxx

Depending on the degree of completion of the work-in-process units, the percentage will be assigned with respect to materials and conversion (labor and overhead) costs to calculate the accurate amount of work done to be matched with the manufacturing costs for the period.

In a JIT environment, where ending and beginning work-in-process and finished-goods inventories are insignificant, there would not exist a significant difference between (1) units completed and (5) amount of work done in the current period only. In a very successful JIT system, even (1) units completed and (3) amount of work done to date may not be very much different.

Accordingly, accountants could forgo the calculation of equivalent units entirely. This will save a tremendous amount of time and cost in the areas of data collection, analysis, and reporting, while the sacrifice in the accuracy of reported data would be marginal.

When JIT is introduced, cycle time is calculated and the uniform plant load is determined in connection with the number of Kanbans discussed in Chapter Three. The cell or plant is redesigned so that all facilities are adjacent to each other. This reduces the time between operations to a minimum. The people who run the cell can pool and share any idle time.

The consequence of these actions are the establishment of a process environment: Almost zero inventory between operations; zero time between operations; and simplification of the entire process. From an accounting perspective, the result is a process system rather than a job-shop system [Johansson, 1986].

Spoilage and Defective Units

As JIT and total quality control concepts are successfully practiced and the spoilage and defect rates are substantially reduced, a separate tracing and accounting for the costs of spoilage in process costing may become unnecessary. Instead of the concepts of normal and abnormal spoilage, all spoilage might be considered abnormal and controllable. The system would no longer tolerate normal spoilage.

Changing Cost Structure

According to Kaplan [1985, p.11], the existing cost and managerial accounting systems were developed in the early part of the twentieth century for a very different type of production environment compared to what we see today. Those systems were designed to closely monitor direct labor costs for mass production of a few standardized items, since direct labor cost was a significant portion of total product cost.

Manufacturing overhead costs, under those systems, are allocated primarily based on direct labor costs. Direct labor content in the production, nevertheless, has decreased dramatically over the years since the 1920s, as companies automated their operations. Kaplan observes that, 70 years ago, overhead might only have been 50-60 percent of direct labor cost. Today most firms' overhead burden rate is above 400-500 percent of direct labor dollars [1985, p.11]. For example, in many electronic products, direct labor accounts for only around four percent of product costs [Linnen, 1983, p.1].

How have cost and managerial accountants adapted to the new environment? Schwarzbach, based on his survey of 112 manufacturing firms, reports that, in general, automated firms and overhead-intensive firms have not modified their cost systems to reflect the significance of overhead costs. Most firms still use direct labor to allocate overhead [1985].

The same report also indicates that most accountants do not validate the relationship between the overhead and the allocation base statistically. They look for a logical relationship but, as they do not test it statistically, it is not surprising that they do not choose different bases as operations change [p.47].

Some changes, nevertheless, are certainly taking place. At H-P, direct labor is no longer accounted for as a separate product cost. With only 3-5 percent of product cost attributed to the direct labor component, accountants and managers see little benefit in standard cost and variance analyses of direct labor. Direct labor is now included in manufacturing overhead [HG & M, 1985, p.60]. This adjustment to the changing nature of operations will reduce a significant amount of cost and effort spent on distinguishing between the two cost categories and between different work orders.

JIT and Cost System Modification

As seen in the above cases, traditional cost systems are not well suited for the implementation of JIT. Some proponents of JIT believe that the elimination of cost accounting would help in a successful and speedy implementation of JIT [Holbrook, 1985].

In Japan, the problem of emphasizing short-term efficiency and cost reduction on the part of cost accountants has been reported to be an obstacle to the implementation of JIT. Dr. Ohno, the father of JIT, has stated that he had to keep cost accountants out of his plant and prevent the knowledge of traditional cost accounting principles from entering into the minds of his manufacturing people [Fox, 1986, p.36].

Present cost accounting systems are too restrictive and complex, according to Holbrook, to be of any value to JIT implementation. The system needs to be modified so that it will be more flexible and simple. Before any modification is made, however, there should be an internal audit of the existing cost system for proper evaluation of the new demands and current capabilities.

A comprehensive view is needed for the internal audit of the cost systems. Therefore, it is desirable to form an audit team made up of managers from various functional areas within the organization [Eiler, Goletz, and Keegan, 1982]. After all, what cost accountants identify, measure, and report on should be understood and accepted by all organizational units affected to promote goal congruence.

JIT and Inventory Valuation

In traditional cost systems, inventory valuation is a major task which requires a substantial amount of time and clerical cost. As JIT simplifies various phases of the firm operations, the number of transactions — materials handling, scheduling, inventory control, and so forth — decreases and inventory level is reduced. This will help the firm simplify inventory valuation to a great extent.

In a previous section of this chapter, we observed the changes caused by the introduction of JIT into the operations of H-P. They treat labor and overhead costs as period expenses now rather than tracing them to specific products.

The problem of doing that for multi-products can be handled as follows: Calculate a historical ratio between labor and work-in-process inventory. When the cycle time is obtained, use the cycle time and the ratio to determine what percentage of labor cost is in the work in process.

Cycle time is also used to differentiate the products that take longer to process than others. This is helpful when multiproducts are involved in a standard costing system. At the end of each month, actual deviations from the standards are observed in aggregate. But the count of cycle time and the observation of what is on the shop floor will enable cost accountants to understand the variances in the processes from month to month [Wright, 1986].

Variable Costing vs. Absorption Costing

Variable costing has been devised to prepare income statements using the contribution-margin approach. Under variable costing, only variable costs — direct materials, direct labor, and variable overhead costs — are included in the product costs. Fixed manufacturing overhead is treated as a period expense. Accordingly, no element of fixed cost is contained in the inventory cost under the variable costing method.

Absorption costing, on the other hand, includes both fixed and variable costs in the calculation of product costs. The product costs consist of direct materials, direct labor, and both variable and fixed overhead costs.

Under absorption costing, therefore, it is possible to artificially generate profit by producing more than the company can sell; the excess inventory units remaining at the end of the period contains the portion of the fixed overhead costs allocated to them. This portion of the cost is deferred to future periods in which the units are sold.

The contribution-margin approach used in variable costing has made it popular for use in decision making, while absorption costing has remained as the method to be employed for external reporting purposes. But the changes in the environment have made variable costing less important. This is because (1) the percentage of variable costs in the total manufacturing cost has decreased, and (2) grouping fixed overhead items together to be charged to the period does not help the company find ways to control rising fixed overhead costs.

Labor cost in an automated manufacturing system tends to become mostly fixed. According to Dilts and Russell [1985], the labor cost that remains in an FMS system represents the cost of individuals performing the initial machine and matérial loading, but only for a single shift of a three-shift operation. For the other two shifts, not much direct labor is needed once the loading has been performed.

In the new environment of managerial accounting, absorption costing therefore becomes the only meaningful costing method. The only significant component of variable manufacturing costs left will be raw materials cost.

Cost Collection in the New Environment

Changes in manufacturing technology have made cost collection easier. In the automated process, machine and product-centered data — details of hour-to-hour and part-to-part manufacturing — are routinely collected for use by the system in scheduling and maintenance. Automated reading devices on parts make continuous tracking of parts possible.

Thus, the cost of acquiring data is substantially reduced as the new technologies are introduced into the system. As personal computers can be used for the necessary analyses of the costs, instead of relying on central information systems department, the whole process of collecting and using cost data becomes simpler [Dilts and Russell, 1985].

The question now becomes at what point cost information should be accumulated. Data accumulation points are no longer at a department level because under JIT, manufacturing is not departmentalized. About 40 percent of the plant is empty under JIT, and the products move from cell to cell very rapidly. In a traditional plant layout, manufacturing is departmentalized: Various types of machinery function in various departments. In the new environment, a plant can make so many different parts and the concept of department is lost [Hronec, 1986].

At what level or in what manner should the information be accumulated and allocated? This issue will be discussed as a separate topic in section 5-4.

Knowledge Workers and Learning Curves

As technological changes take place, the nature of workers and engineers employed in the operations changes. So-called knowledge workers — manufacturing engineers, highly trained operators, quality control personnel, etc. — will replace the conventional work force. These highly-paid professionals are not interchangeable any more.

Although this type of labor is more of a direct nature than indirect, it is primarily fixed. The birth of a whole new breed of professionals raises issues of motivation and performance measurement, among other human resource issues. Chapter Six is devoted to the discussion of performance-related issues in the new environment.

The changes have a significant effect on learning curves also. A learning curve is based on the premise that, as workers become more familiar with repetitive production work, they become more proficient, thereby taking less labor hours to do the job and making fewer mistakes. The decrease in time follows a definite pattern.

The pattern is so regular in many manufacturing industries that the rate of improvement can be reduced to a formula and labor hours can be forecasted with a high degree of accuracy from a learning curve. The curve is usually expressed by its complement. If the rate of reduction is 10 percent, it is a 90 percent curve. Statistical and graphic approaches can be used for actual applications by companies to plan and control labor costs.

The new technologies alter the whole concept of learning curves. The curve no longer has any significance at the machine level in an FMS or CIM setting. Once the system has learned the operation method, it will repeat the task identically each time [Dilts and Russell, 1985]. The reduction in labor hours of workers ceases to be an important issue.

The New Environment and Service Industry

While it is true that the most significant influences of the changing environment are felt in manufacturing industry, service industries are not completely "off limits" either. According to Kaplan [1986a], service industries are going through similar dramatic changes due to the deregulatory force that has occurred in the 1980s.

In Chapter 3 we observed the changes taking place in the transportation industry. Financial services (banking, insurance, etc.), healthcare, and telecommunications industries, Kaplan states, are experiencing significant changes as a result of deregulation also. Companies in these industries function as diverse, multiproduct organizations. For example, banks offer various types of customer services, deposits, and loans. Product costing for the services they sell is done in a fashion very similar to that for manufacturing companies.

In the old regulated environment, Kaplan states, the pricing for these services was done on the basis of all the costs incurred plus markup. A detailed analysis of costs and prices was not necessary due to the restrictions placed on the operations by regulatory agencies. Now the fierce competition in the market forces them to look at the profitability of each service individually.

The companies now have to re-examine their costing and pricing systems so that the systems can provide useful information for long-term as well as short-term managerial decision making. The cost allocation discussion presented in the next section is particularly relevant to that end.

5-4. COST ALLOCATION IN THE NEW ENVIRONMENT

There are two stages in the cost allocation process, according to Kaplan [1986b]. The first stage is the allocation of plantwide overhead costs — utilities, materials handling, inventory management, factory supplies — to various cost centers. The cost pools representing the plantwide services provided by these areas are distributed to manufacturing departments as illustrated in Figure 5.1.

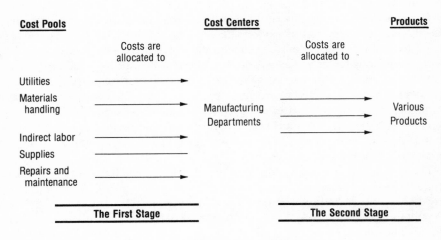

Figure 5.1. The Two Stages of the Cost Allocation Process

As products are routed through those manufacturing departments — cost centers — in the factory, the pool of costs, now traced to each cost center, should be allocated to the products. This is the second stage of the cost allocation process.

The first stage, Kaplan states, is functioning well in most companies. Allocation bases used follow the causation guideline pretty well and no significant problems exist. Utilities and factory supplies could be allocated based on machine hours, indirect labor on labor hours, and so forth.

The problem exists in the second stage. The single measure of activity — direct labor hours or machine hours — currently used by most companies for the second-stage allocation does not produce product cost information useful for managerial decision making. The basic flaw is that direct labor hours or machine hours does not correctly represent the amount of resources consumed by the product during the routing process.

A dangerous assumption made in this kind of cost allocation is that the costs are driven by that single variable, labor or machine hours. It is very unlikely that this is actually the case. Rather, Kaplan and other authors argue, *transactions* generate overhead costs.

For example, purchasing department cost is driven by the number of purchase orders processed, information systems department cost by the amount of bills, parts, and materials to track and handle, setup cost by the number of setups and hours they take, and engineering department cost by the number of engineering change orders. Those represent the types of transactions that drive overhead costs up to the level which can be seen in the environments of today and tomorrow.

Homogeneous Cost Drivers

The present cost allocation problems, caused by relying on a single allocation basis such as direct labor hours or machine hours, have led to miscosting and mispricing of products. A significant portion of overhead costs are allocated to wrong product lines and units just because they use longer labor hours which have very little bearing on how overhead costs are really driven up in the new environment.

To overcome the problems, it may be possible to find a set of cost pools for which there is only one cost driver, i.e., the factor that explains why that level of costs have been incurred. There may be dozens of cost pool sets. When the goal of finding homogeneous drivers is achieved, then perform the calculations on personal computers using a spreadsheet software. For even dozens of those drivers, the calculations would not be a problem these days thanks to the availability of PCs and softwares.

One example: When a product is routed through different processes in the factory, consider how many machine hours in each process it requires. The product generates a demand for machine hours that cause a certain pool of costs to increase. Machine hour is the driver here, used to allocate the costs in that pool. Costs related to setup could be in another pool, and so forth.

Cost accountants must escape the confined thinking that costs vary with the changes in the volume of production. There are many costs in the plants that vary not with the volume of production but with transactions. The reason why JIT is so effective in reducing costs is that it reduces transactions.

Many practitioners agree with this reasoning. Coran states that when a shop is broken down into the various processes of production centers, different overhead rates should be used on the basis of the level of technology and the types of machines, services, and support used. The present cost accounting systems, however, tag all direct labor with the same average overhead rate [1986].

New Types of Costs and their Distributions

Technological changes create a focused subplant with U-shaped machine cells within the plant. Different types of costs are now identified at different levels:

At the plant level — Factory administration and space costs.

At the focused subplant level — Utilities, engineering, and directly-attributable administration and some interest costs.

At the cell level — Team labor (instead of traditional direct labor), direct space and machine charges, and maintenance.

One way to break down the overhead pool is to examine and classify costs based on the value-added concept [Hronec, 1986; Johansson, 1986]. In a JIT setting, there are very few short-term variable costs and very few fixed costs within the relevant range of manufacturing activity. This ambiguity is observed in a traditional setting also, but JIT makes it more pervasive.

Hronec and Johansson suggest that if costs add value to the product, those costs should be accumulated at the cell level. The costs of the cell can be distributed to products according to the cell time a product takes within each cell. "Inventory velocity" (how fast the inventory moves through the cell) will be the key measurement used [Hronec, 1986].

If costs do not add value, as in the case of materials handling costs, then determine the service or support level and allocate to the cells later. Reporting costs on the basis of whether they add value or not will draw the management's attention to the nonvalue-added costs. This helps the company in its attempt to eliminate the waste from the manufacturing process, by focusing on the critical nature of costs, Hronec states.

The value-added concept can be incorporated in the process of finding homogeneous cost drivers mentioned above by Kaplan. The two classes — value-added or not — can be separately listed, at least, when cost allocation results are reported, if they are not used in the identification of homogeneous cost drivers.

5-5. COST CONTROL IN THE NEW ENVIRONMENT

Real-Time Information

Technological advances reduce the time required in the production cycle, which calls for timely information to support the process. In the new manufacturing environment, most of the manufacturing data never leave the system. They are not used for managerial decision making yet, except for local process decisions. According to Brimson [1986], much of the information that was processed in a batch mode must now be processed real time to be useful.

Increased availability and accuracy of shop-floor data should help management accountants evaluate and control many indirect costs in a direct manner. The definition of indirect costs may also need to be reviewed while cost drivers mentioned in the previous section are identified. This is because the best way to control costs is to control cost drivers, which are actually transactions.

Overhead Cost Control in the Long Run

Based on a survey of manufacturers' operations, Miller and Vollman report that 20 to 40 percent of all transactions are change transactions, 25 to 40 percent are design and quality transactions, 10 to 20 percent are logistical transactions, and 10 to 20 percent are balancing transactions [1985]. Citing a study made by Arthur Andersen & Co., Brimson lists, as individual cost drivers, engineering change orders, space utilization, forecast errors, master schedule changes, inventory levels, product design and lack of interchangeable components, multiple bills of materials, etc. [1986].

In order to control costs, the transactions can be eliminated, integrated, stabilized, or automated. JIT eliminates transactions. Vendor scheduling, guaranteed employment, and movement toward repetitive manufacturing stabilize transactions. Bar coding and paperless factories automate transactions.

A New System and Management Accountant

Extensive automation may reduce, rather than increase, the need for measurement and control points. Data on the degree of completion in many parts are kept in the internal logic processes of the machines, or such knowledge may not be needed due to the high integrity of the automated linkages. A management accountant's traditional authority over the basic data is taken away [Johansson, 1986].

While the need for better real-time information for process control demands a more active role of management accountants, the above reality might to some extent put a limit on the same role. According to Johansson, the automated floor, nevertheless, enables a management accountant to:

- simulate the effects of material changes,
- update costs fast (even on-line),
- monitor the progress of individual work orders,
- control inventory on-line,
- evaluate the cost implication of engineering changes, and
- understand production variances precisely and easily.

To utilize the automated facilities to the maximum, management accountants also need to develop multiple standards corresponding to the need for sufficient diversity in the product mix, which will ensure that all machines are used [Dilts and Russell, 1985]. The cost standards, however, must be restated in terms of new cost allocation bases. While manufacturing managers have to cope with the difficulty of controlling the operation of the new system because they can no longer use informal procedures based on their experience with direct labor hours, accountants experience the same difficulty: little of the usual data for calculating standard costs is available.

Since computerized manufacturing is so new to many companies, no factory can initially obtain all the needed historical information. Therefore, cost standards must be determined primarily by intuitive estimate. This, of course, can not be relied upon for such cost components as rework and maintenance [Gerwin, 1982].

The management accountant's difficult task of coping with the rapidly changing environment is more severe in high-tech fields. Most manufactured goods (and services) spend most of their lives in the last two stages — mature and decline stages — which are the domain of most management accounting tools. High-tech products, by contrast, spend most of their lives in the first two stages — start-up and growth stages.

Management accountants are knowledgeable about the mature and decline stages which have characteristics of stability, long production runs, and cost control emphasis. But the high tech's continual operations in the start-up and growth stages force the R & D function to merge with the production function. Consequently, it becomes very difficult for management accountants to compile the data set needed for setting standards [Littrel, 1984].

Some changes, in the meantime, facilitate management accountant's work. For example, by integrating MRP with cost accounting, planned costs and performances are available as normal system outputs in the form of reports or shop documentation. Actual performance data with costed variances by type, operation, or order is available directly from the cost system or through online inquiry into the data base on a CRT terminal.

5-6. CONCLUSION

In this chapter we have looked at various problems and new opportunities the environmental changes bring to management accountants' work. These challenges must be responded to with innovative restructuring of the management accounting systems appropriate for the area. Management accountants must continually re-examine the needs and capabilities of the existing systems and be prepared to accommodate potential changes.

Influences of the changing environment on product costing systems and control have been found to be very significant, rather dramatic, in light of the short period of time they have taken [Lee, 1985]. This is in striking contrast to the gradual and moderate changes which have taken place in management accounting over the last several decades. Next decade will certainly see a wave of revolutionary changes in the theory and practice of cost accounting.

The influences on management control and performance measurement of the changing environment will be discussed in Chapter 6.

REFERENCES

Anthony, R.N., J. Dearden, and N. Bedford, *Management Control Systems,* Fifth Edition (Homewood, Illinois: Richard D. Irwin, Inc., 1984).

Brimson, J.A., "How Advanced Manufacturing Technologies Are Reshaping Cost Management," *Management Accounting* (March 1986), pp. 25-29.

Coran, M.S., "How Government Contractors Approach Factory Automation: The Accounting Implications," *Cost Accounting for the 90s* (Montvale, N.J.: National Association of Accountants, 1986), pp. 93-97.

Dickey, R., ed., *Accountants' Cost Handbook* (New York: Ronald Press, 1960).

Dilts, D.M. and G.W. Russell, "Accounting for the Factory of the Future," *Management Accounting* (April 1985), pp. 34-40.

Dopuch, N., J.G. Birnberg, and J. Demski, *Cost Accounting,* Second Edition (New York: Harcourt Brace Jovanovich, Inc., 1974).

Eiler, R.G., W.K. Goletz, and D.P. Keegan, "Is Your Cost Accounting Up to Date?" *Harvard Business Review* (July-August 1982), pp. 133-139.

Fox, R.E., "Cost Accounting: Asset or Liability?" *Journal of Accounting and EDP* (Winter 1986), pp. 31-37.

Gerwin, D., "Do's and Don'ts of Computerized Manufacturing," *Harvard Business Review* (March-April 1982), pp. 107-116.

Holbrook, W., "Practical Accounting Advice for Just-in-Time Production," *Journal of Accounting and EDP* (Fall 1985), pp. 42-47.

Hronec, S.M., "The Effects of Manufacturing Productivity on Cost Accounting and Management Reporting," *Cost Accounting for the 90s* (Montvale, N.J.: National Association of Accountants, 1986), pp. 117-128.

Hunt, R., L. Garrett, and C.M. Merz, "Direct Labor Cost Not Always Relevant at H-P," *Management Accounting* (February 1985), pp. 58-62.

Johansson, H.J., "The Effect of Zero Inventories on Cost (Just-in-Time)," *Cost Accounting for the 90s* (National Association of Accountants), pp. 141-148.

Kaplan, R.S., "The Evolution of Management Accounting," *The Accounting Review* (July 1984), pp. 390-418.

_____, "Cost Accounting: A Revolution in the Making," (An Interview) *Corporate Accounting* (Spring 1985), pp. 10-16.

_____, "Introduction" (1986a) and "Strategic Cost Analysis" (1986b) in *Cost Accounting for the 90s* (Montvale, N.J.:National Association of Accountants, 1986), pp. 7-10 and 129-138.

Kuhn, T., *The Structure of Scientific Revolutions*, Second Edition (University of Chicago Press, 1962).

Lee, J.Y., "The Quiet Revolution in Inventory Management," *FE: The Magazine for Financial Executives* (December 1985), pp. 37- 40.

Linnen, P., "No Inventory - No Cost Systems," *Hewlett-Packard Financial Notes* (September 1983), p.1.

Littrel, E.K., "The High Tech Challenge to Management Accounting," *Management Accounting* (October 1984), pp.33-36.

Miller, J.G. and T.E. Vollman, "The Hidden Factory," *Harvard Business Review* (September-October 1985), pp. 142-150.

Sauers, D.G., "Analyzing Inventory Systems," *Management Accounting* (May 1986), pp. 30-36.

Schwarzbach, H.R., "The Impact of Automation on Accounting for Indirect Costs," *Management Accounting* (December 1985), pp. 45-50.

Seglund, R. and S. Ibarreche, "Just-in-Time: The Accounting Implications," *Management Accounting* (August 1984), pp. 43-45.

Wright, V., "The Effect of Zero Inventories on Cost (Just-in-Time)," *Cost Accounting for the 90s* (Montvale, N.J.: National Association of Accountants, 1986), pp.156-164.

SUGGESTED ADDITIONAL READINGS

Brooks, H., "Business Gets a Grip on Inventories," *Business Week* (May 14, 1984), pp. 38-39.

Davis, J., "These 7 Accounting Weaknesses Can Harm Your Company!" *Management Accounting* (August 1983), pp. 55-56.

Hall, R. and J. Nakane, "Management Specs for a Stockless Production," *Harvard Business Review* (May-June 1983), pp. 84-91.

Harbour, J., "Just in Time, Not Just in Case," *Corporate Accounting* (Spring 1985), pp. 5-8.

Kaplan, R.S., "Yesterday's Accounting Undermines Production," *Harvard Business Review* (July-August 1984), pp. 95-101.

Keys, D.E., "Six Problems in Accounting for N/C Machines," *Management Accounting* (November 1986), pp. 38-47.

King, B., L. Krajewski, and L. Ritaman, "Manufacturing Performance - Pulling the Right Levers," *Harvard Business Review* (March-April 1984), pp. 143-152.

Lee, J.Y., "Inventory Management Techniques: Eastern Perspective," *National Public Accountant* (August 1986), pp. 30-33.

Melnyk, S.A. and R.F. Gonzalez, "MRP II: The Early Returns Are In," *Production and Inventory Management* (First Quarter 1985), pp. 124-136.

Sadhwani, A.T., M.H. Sarhan, and D. Kiringoda, "Just-in-Time: An Inventory System Whose Time Has Come," *Management Accounting* (December 1985), pp. 36-44.

Taussig, R. and W.L. Shaw, "Accounting for Productivity: A Practical Approach," *Management Accounting* (May 1985), pp.48-52.

CHAPTER SIX

The Influences of the Changing Environment on Management Control and Performance Measurement

6-1. THE NEW ENVIRONMENT AND THE POSITIVE PERFORMANCE MODEL

According to traditional cost accounting principles, cost reductions and higher efficiency should lead to higher profits for the company. The cost of goods manufactured decreases at local production stations and processes due to cost reductions and efficiency improvements, which in turn results in greater profits.

In the late 1970s, many U.S. companies started aggressive programs to revitalize their manufacturing functions. These efforts to regain a competitive edge have been directed at reducing costs and eliminating waste and inefficiency and have been quite successful. The success, nevertheless, has not brought higher profits to the companies [Skinner, 1986]. Why not? This problem has frustrated executives who have spent enormous amounts of effort and time on improving productivity by doing the above.

Taiichi Ohno, the developer of JIT, has reportedly mentioned that cost accounting has been his biggest obstacle to the implementation of JIT at Toyota [Fox, 1984]. According to Fox, Ohno stated that cost accountants in Japan, like their Western counterparts, believe in high efficiency, low-cost operations, and adherence to traditional cost accounting principles, none of which could explain why JIT was so successful. Ohno reportedly had to keep the cost accountants out of the plant, and had to "prevent the knowledge of cost accounting from entering into the minds of" his people.

As radical changes take place in the environment of managerial accounting, the traditional cost accounting principles sometimes are in conflict with the managerial actions required to compete in the marketplace and generate profits, as illustrated in the above two examples. We, as a profession, are challenged by these developments to come up with a new framework to provide meaningful explanations about the new phenomena in the environment.

Although they have not been formally incorporated into a coherent theory set, there have been fragmentary statements and explanations offered by practitioners and academicians which, if integrated together, can provide a meaningful set of consistent answers to most of the questions raised about the performance of the firms in the new environment. In this chapter, those pieces of knowledge will be integrated into a new framework, which represents the positive performance model.

First, we will need to understand the background of the issues, which will be discussed in the following sections. Second, we will look at the positive performance model. Third, some further considerations of the issues will be presented.

6-2. MANAGEMENT CONTROL AND PERFORMANCE MEASUREMENT

Every organization has goals either explicit or implicit, which represent a broad, fairly timeless statement of what the organization desires to achieve. To attain the goals, the organization needs strategies that include policies, programs, and plans. Management control systems are designed and operated for the implementation of those strategies [Anthony, Dearden, and Bedford, 1984, hereafter AD & B, Chapter 3].

Management control systems (MCS) rely on performance measurement to facilitate planning and to motivate managers to achieve goals. For meaningful performance measurements, MCS need suitable measures which are explained by variables. Strategic variables, which are regarded as the key factors in explaining success or failure of the organization, include competitors' actions and changes in industry (environmental variables); market share, product quality, and delivery performance (functional variables); and return on investment and inventory turnover (asset variables).

These variables can change quickly, and their changes are not easy to predict. They need constant attention of managers since management controls that focus on the wrong variables produce disappointing results.

6-3. A NEW LOOK AT EFFICIENCY AND PRODUCTIVITY

Efficiency represents primarily a ratio of output to input. Effectiveness expresses the relationship between output and the organization's objectives — goals made more specific in terms of the ends to achieve within a certain time period [AD & B, Chapters 3 and 5]. The following diagram will help to express the relationships among these:

Input ——————————— Output ——————————— Objectives
(Efficiency)　　　　　　　　(Effectiveness)

U.S. industry's frustration, according to Skinner[1986], has been caused originally by focusing on wrong targets — cost reduction and elimination of waste and inefficiency. Skinner states that the way managers define productivity improvement and the tools they use to achieve it have been wrong. U.S. managers mainly have been concerned with direct labor efficiency when direct labor costs exceed 10 percent of sales in only a few industries. By focusing on the efficiency of factory workers at the individual and departmental levels, the programs have detracted attention from the crucial manufacturing strategy and structure.

Managers under relentless pressure to boost productivity resist innovation, since they know any changes in process will interfere with their attempt to meet the weekly cost performance targets. This preoccupation with productivity maximization forces managers to adopt short-term, operational views, which alienate the work force. Based on this analysis, Skinner proposes that managers focus on a wider set of objectives than cost and efficiency.

While efficiency is measured by relating input resources consumed to outputs achieved, effectiveness represents how much those outputs contribute to the objectives. Accordingly, to achieve the desired objectives with minimum input resources, emphasis of management should be on both efficiency and effectiveness, provided they move in the same direction, as discussed in the section where the formulation of the positive performance model is presented.

In recent years, U.S. industry has put too much emphasis on efficiency and cost reductions — at the expense of effectiveness — reducing defects, lead times, and time it takes to respond to market changes. Somehow, managers have neglected to make a direct connection from efficiency to effectiveness. They should have been more concerned with the issue of how to extend local productivity to global, or organizational, optimization of resource utilization.

Conventional Production Efficiency

Conventional production wisdom calls for big batches and long production runs. "When a troublesome operation is running well, why not produce a lot of parts so that it doesn't need to be run again for a long time?" This logic, according to Fox [1986], advocates big batches and long runs. In a conventional manufacturing setting, frequent setups and changeovers result in more machine down time, more indirect labor hours, and less efficient use of direct labor.

In that setting, long runs will certainly lead to better utilization of direct labor for a given amount of indirect labor. Short production runs coupled with frequent changeovers will make the performance of production managers look poor. As a result, the application of innovative management techniques such as JIT and OPT requires a reevaluation of performance evaluation systems as well.

JIT, OPT, and Efficiency

Under the concept of OPT, high efficiency at local stations leads to lower profit performance for the company as a whole, when bottlenecks exist somewhere along the process. This is because that high efficiency creates excess inventory locally, which increases operating expenses, as discussed previously. In that case, local efficiency is not translated into higher profitability for the company.

In a JIT setting, quite often workers sit idle until they are told otherwise. Idle time is not regarded as evil. Lot sizes are small, and plant work load, determined in connection with Kanbans, is uniform. When product quality is aggressively planned into the entire production process, uniform plant load (UPL) becomes a reality based on the balancing of production among different production cells. Furthermore, defect rate is lowered to a few per million, and quality rejects are very rare.

The production function is viewed in a JIT setting from a perspective which is entirely different from conventional perspectives. JIT seeks a more global optimization of the production and distribution network. It avoids local optimizations, such as EOQs, at subsystems that may be realized at the expense of the larger system. By accepting short-term diseconomies — reducing inventory to below optimal EOQ levels — it can decrease the long-term total costs [Sauers, 1986].[1]

Conventional production efficiency cannot be used as the criterion for performance evaluation at the cells in the plant using JIT. This is because UPL is determined based on marketing considerations: Lower demand in the market will lead to less UPL, which in turn means under-applied overhead. When manufacturing does not change UPL, it should not be held responsible for unfavorable variances.

Automation and Efficiency

In an automated plant, individual efficiency has very little importance. When an FMS is installed, for example, you no longer find jobs passing through different work centers which allocate costs to the jobs as they proceed operation by operation. Rather, product items emerge piece by piece apparently with very similar costs as they are turned out of the automated processes. The costs, which used to be mainly variable, become more and more volume and product independent [Johansson, 1985].

In this type of production setting, individual workers perform their duties as the job environment dictates. They are supposed to adhere to the schedule determined according to the overall production needs. Efficiency measured by the deviations from the standards on an individual basis is not the major issue.

6-4. THE POSITIVE PERFORMANCE MODEL

The Model

Based on the observations which have been made so far on the efficiency, productivity, and profits in different manufacturing environments, the following thesis is presented: The essence of management control in the new environment should be a focus on positive performance, and performance measurement must be done within this framework.

The focus on positive performance reflects an explicit preference for the optimum utilization of resources for the company as a whole; for compliance with the

---

[1] The long-run total costs of a manufacturer, according to Sauers, should include production costs, inventory costs, and the costs of customer dissatisfaction caused by long lead times, poor product quality, stockouts, etc. The last type of costs, which are under the control of the manufacturing manager, will increase warranty expense and adversely affect sales revenue.

schedule within the entire manufacturing structure; for the employees' positive contribution to the attainment of the company's goals and objectives through cooperative efforts; and for making direct and consistent connections to the company's goals when managers make decisions on operations-related actions. The model is presented in Figure 6.1.

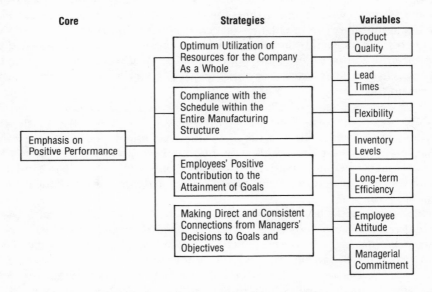

Figure 6.1 The Positive Performance Model

The positive performance represents the actions taken by managers and employees that will contribute positively to the attainment of goals. Local efficiency quite often leads to the wasteful accumulation of inventory and efforts by managers to boost efficiency would frequently alienate the work force, which is detrimental to the long-term profitability. Effectiveness, unless proper objectives are established within the system, would not contribute positively to attaining profit goals.

The Differences from Conventional Models

The positive performance model (PPM) is different from conventional management control models (for the manufacturing function) in the following aspects:

1. In the conventional models, efficiency is always assumed to be a positive force that contributes to goal attainment — increased profits. We have seen in the current and previous chapters that this assumption is not valid when there are bottlenecks in the production line, not to mention the negative impact on the morale of the work force when undue pressure is exerted to meet the efficiency target.

Efficiency, according to PPM, contributes to goal attainment only when it becomes positive performance, as required by the strategy of optimum utilization of resources for the company as a whole. If, for example under JIT or OPT, a cell in the plant operates when it is not supposed to, the conventional efficiency of better machine utilization reported on the weekly performance report actually means higher cost and lower profit for the company.

2. In the conventional models, effectiveness, which represents how much the output contributes to the objectives, is used rather rigidly when a company's achievement is evaluated. When a company's objectives are erroneously set from a short-term viewpoint, effectiveness is translated as cost reductions at local points in the short run but higher total costs in the long run.

   This is evidenced by an example where short-term cost reductions led to customer dissatisfaction because of poor product quality and slow reponse to changes in consumer tastes. (See note 1 on page 66 for Sauers's statement on the long-run total costs.)

   PPM looks at effectiveness as a very flexible term. It recognizes the fragile nature of the objectives when viewed from a long-term perspective. As the environment undergoes changes, the set of objectives established by the organization under given circumstances should be modified accordingly. Under PPM, effectiveness becomes positive performance only when the objectives have been tested in the new environment to be viable in the attainment of the organization's goals.

3. PPM recognizes the limitations of individualistic performance in the process of attaining the organization's goals. Excellence in individual performance ("superstar" performance), which is promoted under conventional management control theories, is not of paramount importance under PPM.

   What makes a company profitable in the long run is the formulation and implementation of sound manufacturing strategy and structure, not individuals' superior performance. Individual employees and departments cannot be better than the structure within which they operate.

   This is why compliance with the schedule within the entire manufacturing structure is more valued than individuals' superb performance in terms of narrowly defined efficiency and effectiveness under PPM. Performance as a member in a group — cell, plant, or company — is more emphasized than a superstar performance as an individual when actions are evaluated to determine whether they can be regarded as positive performance.

4. Although conventional models deal with the issue of connecting managers' decisions with the goals and objectives of the organization, the implicit assumption is that the connection can be made in regular time intervals, probably once a year when each budgetary unit goes over the assigned tasks and allowed expenses. In the new environment, according to PPM, organizations can not afford to do that. Managers must make direct and consistent connections between their decisions and the organizational goals and objectives, since objectives may need to be reevaluated a lot more frequently than before as changes take place in the new environment at a significantly faster pace.

The Strategies and Variables

In order to plan for the implementation of the strategies which were discussed in the previous two sections and presented in Figure 6.1, and to motivate managers to maximize their efforts to achieve goals, appropriate measures of performance — variables — are needed. As changes take place in the environment, the variables used should change accordingly.

The variables that have been used by U.S. companies are short-term cost reductions, short-term efficiency, and other short-term financial performance measures. These variables had been originally developed by companies in their attempt to derive optimal decisions in a stable and predictable environment. The realistic cost structure, especially that of fixed overhead, and the uncertainty in demand and delivery times were not considered [Kaplan, 1983].

U.S. companies, according to Kaplan, have been trying to find optimal policies under existing conditions, while their Japanese counterparts have encouraged managers to intervene actively in the production process under the assumption that the existing conditions can be changed. They have concentrated their efforts on improving quality, reducing setup times, increasing manufacturing flexibility, and overcoming restrictive workforce rules.

The variables that are needed in the new environment should be compatible with the new strategies formulated above. The list of the new variables, although not exhaustive, includes product quality, lead times, flexibility, inventory levels, long-term efficiency, employee attitude, and managerial commitment. These variables will be further discussed in the next section where performance measurement models are presented.

6-5. THE MEASUREMENT OF POSITIVE PERFORMANCE

A company's management control system in the new environment should be supportive of the new manufacturing strategies. The management control system relies on performance measurement in the whole process of planning and implementation of the strategies. Accordingly, proper performance measurement is of paramount importance in accomplishing a company's goals.

In the above section, the positive performance is proposed as the concept to be used in the new environment to evaluate actions taken by managers and employees. Then, how should the positive performance be measured? The measurement issue is discussed in this section.

Measurement: At the Individual Level or Group Level?

Measuring individual performance and rewarding individual excellence is the basic foundation for responsibility accounting. Merit system, based on individuals' efficiency in their work, has certainly helped U.S. companies attain higher productivity. The emphasis on individual performance, nevertheless, should be reevaluated in the new environment.

As observed so far, in a JIT setting individuals' performance is dictated by the uniform plant load (UPL) and the production schedule. Individual worker productivity is irrelevant. Setup time, for example, when used as a performance measure, should be measured at the cell level, not at the individual worker level. Machine downtime which is often used in a conventional production setting to indicate the level of efficiency in utilizing facilities, can not be used as a performance measure.

Sometimes workers are not supposed to operate the machine under the JIT and OPT system.

In an automated manufacturing process as well, the whole system is so integrated and controlled by computers that individuals' performance would be confined to following the preprogrammed flow of the process. The system's productivity would be affected very little by the varying degrees of individual employees' ability, once the employees acquire the proficiency needed to operate in that setting.

The emphasis in the new environment, therefore, should be placed on the group performance. The well-coordinated efforts at the cell level or plant level should be important in accomplishing goals. Conflicts among employees and processes would produce a lot more serious consequences in the new environment than it did in the conventional environment. The measurement of positive performance in this context should indicate the desirability of instituting group incentives, rather than piecework incentives.[2]

Global Optimization and Loose Evaluation

In a JIT, OPT, or automated production setting, global optimization of the whole production system is sought. Local optimizations, such as EOQs, are not emphasized at all, since from a long-term viewpoint short-term diseconomies can

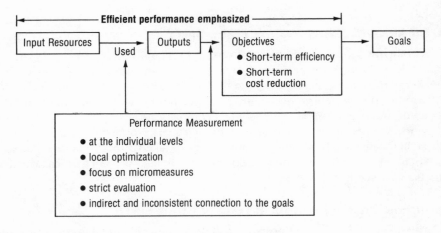

Figure 6.2. A Conventional Performance Measurement Model

be tolerated in order to expose process inefficiencies and thereby reduce the total system costs in the long run [Sauers, 1986].

For the smooth implementation of the global optimization strategies, however, the organization needs the positive attitude and commitment of the employees and

---

[2] JIT and automation have dramatically increased the velocity of throughput. Therefore, the accountant's ability to track the pieces is questionable even when the need to measure individual performances is justified [Sauers, 1986; Johansson, 1986].

managers. In a conventional performance measurement model, there is no emphasis on the need to promote these attributes. As illustrated in Figure 6.2, a conventional model would rely on micromeasures designed to evaluate how much contributions to the objectives of short-term efficiency and cost reductions have been made. The evaluation would also be made in a strict fashion on each individual workers and departments.

The employee's positive attitude and commitment to the organization cannot be promoted in an organization where the members are like strangers. In a typical U.S. company, there has been too much reliance on quantifiable, measurable criteria for performance evaluation. The lack of sufficient consideration of qualitative measures and intangible factors has not helped U.S. companies forge strong binds with the employees who can develop human relationships that will lead to fine coordination of activities, cooperation among employees, and increased productivity.[3]

In the process of measuring positive performance, one would be tempted to experiment with explicit operational performance measures on those variables mentioned above — product quality, short lead times, enhanced flexibility, lower inventory levels, long-term efficiency, etc. Many have already proposed to quantify those variables and report them.[4]

Although fair evaluation of performance is the backbone of a successful management control system, the ultimate utility of attempting to quantify all variables is questionable in light of the organization's need to develop a community of employees who are supportive of the organizational efforts to accomplish goals.

For example, inventory reduction is easily quantified. The benefits of improved quality can also be measured to some extent by looking at surrogate values such as reduced warranty expense. But when defects are measured in parts per million, what actual benefits can a company reap by measuring the quality improvement of 0.00001 %? Also, if a strict measurement of lead time is in force, then cells may hesitate stopping production lines when minor defects occur and may postpone the necessary maintenance in order to show a shorter lead time.

In order to promote positive attitude and commitment of employees including lower-level managers, a tight control employing short-term performance measures should be avoided. Operating measures shown in Figure 6.1 and Figure 6.3 would be helpful when obtained and reported, but a heavy reliance on these measures is not desirable.

Instead, companies are advised to show concern for employees and practice it over an extended period of time. This will help the company earn their commitment [Steers, 1977; Hatvany and Pucik, 1981]. High commitment per se, however, may have only a limited effect on performance. To transform commitment into productive effort, a company needs to articulate a unique company philosophy [Ouchi and Price, 1978; Scott, 1966].

A unique company philosophy, according to Scott, facilitates the transformation since it gives a clear picture of the organization's goals, providing direction for

---

[3] See Ouchi's book on Theory Z for examples of U.S. companies which have succeeded in developing a community of employees who have those desirable attributes [Ouchi, 1981].

[4] See Brimson [1986], Johansson [1986], and Holbrook [1985], among others.

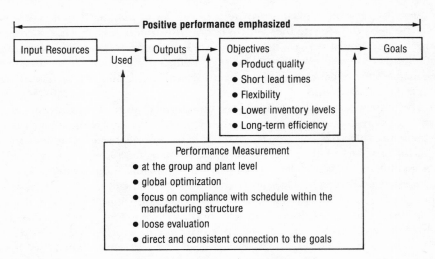

Figure 6.3. The Measurement of Positive Performance.

employees. The philosophy, well communicated to employees and visibly supported in management's behavior, may also serve as an elegant informational device for providing a form of control because it offers managers an all-purpose basic theory of how the firm should be managed [Hatvany and Pucik, 1981; Ouchi and Price, 1978].

Positive Performance: the Answer for the Success of JIT and the Confusion over Productivity Programs

At the beginning of this chapter, we looked at two cases on productivity, efficiency, and profitability: The confusion of many U.S. companies that have tried various productivity programs and Ohno's inability to explain the success of his JIT. Now that we have discussed the positive performance concept, we can suggest one answer to those questions.

JIT and OPT work because they yield positive performance. Efficiency or effectiveness alone do not explain why "not working" is preferred to "working for efficiency's sake." Efficiency or effectiveness alone cannot account for the zero or marginal increase in earnings when productivity increase is substantial. Additional increase in outputs and productivity is translated into higher long-term profits only when the increase in outputs and productivity is positive performance. Positive performance is achieved when performance is connected to the goals of the organization directly and consistently.

6-6. CONCLUSION

In this chapter we looked at the conflict between the traditional cost accounting and management control principles and the managerial actions required to compete in the market with competitors as radical changes take place in the environment of managerial accounting. There should be a fundamental departure from the philosophy dominating conventional performance models. The new paradigm may not have to abandon the existing theoretical frameworks, but it would need to apply different concepts to the area of performance evaluation.

Changes expected to be made in other related areas of management accounting will be discussed in Chapter 7.

REFERENCES

Anthony, R.N., J. Dearden and N. Bedford, *Management Control Systems,* Fifth Edition (Homewood, Illinois: Richard D. Irwin, Inc., 1984).

Brimson, J.A., "How Advanced Manufacturing Technologies Are Reshaping Cost Management," *Management Accounting* (March 1986), pp.25-29.

Fox, R.E., "Main Bottleneck on the Factory Floor?" *Management Review* (November 1984), pp.55-61.

—————, "Cost Accounting: Asset or Liability?" *Journal of Accounting and EDP* (Winter 1986), pp.31-37.

Hatvany, N. and V. Pucik, "An Integrated Management System: Lessons from the Japanese Experience," *Academy of Management Review* (July 1981), pp.469-478.

Holbrook, W.,"Practical Accounting Advice for Just-in-Time Production," *Journal of Accounting and EDP* (Fall 1985), pp. 42-47.

Johansson, H., "The Revolution in Cost Accounting," *P & IM Review and APICS News* (January 1985), pp.42-46.

—————, "The Effect of Zero Inventories on Cost," *Cost Accounting for the 90s* (Montvale, N.J.:National Association of Accountants, 1986), pp.141-156.

Kaplan, R.S., "Measuring Manufacturing Performance: A New Challenge for Managerial Accounting Research," *The Accounting Review* (October 1983), pp.686-705.

Ouchi, W.G., Theory Z: *How American Business Can Meet the Japanese Challenge* (Menlo Park, CA.: Addison-Wesley Publishing Co., 1981).

————— and R. Price, "Hierarchies, Clans, and Theory Z: A New Perspective on Organization Development," *Organizational Dynamics* (Autumn 1978), pp.24-44.

Sauers, D.G., "Analyzing Inventory Systems," *Management Accounting* (May 1986), pp. 30-36.

Scott, W.E., "Activation Theory and Task Design," *Organizational Behavior and Human Performance* (September 1966), pp.3-30.

Skinner, W., "The Productivity Paradox," *Harvard Business Review* (July-August 1986), pp. 55-59.

Steers, R.M., "Antecedents and Outcomes of Organizational Commitment," *Administrative Science Quarterly* (March 1977), pp.46-56.

SUGGESTED ADDITIONAL READINGS

Business Week, "A Work Revolution in U.S. Industry" (May 16, 1983), pp. 100-110.

Gibb, P., "Appraisal Goals and Controls," *Personnel Journal* (August 1985), pp. 89-93.

Lanza, P., "Team Appraisals," *Personnel Journal* (March 1985), pp. 47-51.

Matsuno, S. and W.A. Stoever, "Japanese Boss, American Employees," *The Wharton Magazine* (Fall 1982), pp.45-48.

Monden, Y., *Toyota Production System* (Institute of Industrial Engineers, 1983).

Nave, J.L., "'Z' from Theory to Practice," *Management World* (May 1983), pp. 10-12.

Rohlen, T.P., For Harmony and Strength: *Japanese White-Collar Organization in Anthropological Perspective* (Berkeley, CA.: University of California Press, 1974).

Takeuchi, H., "Productivity: Learning from the Japanese," *California Management Review* (Summer 1981), pp. 5-18.

CHAPTER SEVEN

The Influences of the Changing Environment on Managerial Accounting: Special Topics

7-1. THE IMPACT ON HUMAN RESOURCE ACCOUNTING

The Japanese management practices and the Theory Z which were discussed in previous chapters certainly have appeal in the new environment where positive attitude and commitment of employees are needed for positive performance. These practices have an impact on managerial accounting, especially in the area of human resource accounting.

The new practices represent an entirely new way of thinking. Instead of the typical management-worker conflict found in U.S. industry, a spirit of teamwork is promoted from top management to entry-level workers. One of the key strategies used for this purpose is the development of a set of employment practices that price and allocate labor according to intraorganizational rules and procedures rather than according to market demand and supply conditions, which is referred to as an internal labor market in the economic literature [Doeringer and Piore, 1971].

Internal Labor Market

Internal labor market (ILM) is defined as a method for governing the wage setting and job classification of employees, which is irrespective of external demand. Wages and job classifications are determined through intraorganizational guidelines. Wages are set by the company to encourage long tenure of their employees and job security is promised. Another expression of the firm's commitment to the employee is the amount of training invested in each worker. The firm provides on-the-job training in every aspect of the production process.

The implication of the well-developed ILM is that it decreases the company's dependency on environmental conditions. Employees are hired for the entry-level positions and promotions come entirely from within the organization. The philosophy behind an ILM is to secure a labor force for long-term employment and develop the human resources to match the needs of the organization.

Human Resource Accounting and the New Environment

A human resource accounting (HRA) system is an information system which has been proposed to be used to help companies manage human resources more effectively. The HRA system treats employees as assets and accounts for these assets in the same manner as other physical assets, i.e. capitalizes them for their expected useful lives.

The development of an HRA system depends largely on an accurate measure of the value of employees to an organization. Two theories, one on individual value and the other on group value, have been proposed for the measurement.

The individual value theory is based on the assumption that the value of an organization's human resources is equivalent to the sum of the values of each employee. According to Flamholtz [1974], two major factors determine the individual value: the value an organization can realize from an individual's future services and the probability an individual will remain with the organization.

As new developments take place in the environment at a rapid pace and the importance of teamwork and cooperation among employees is recognized as crucial in accomplishing organizational goals, the above-mentioned assumption of the individual theory seems to be facing a tough test. The GM-Toyota joint venture at Fremont, California, for example, has had a huge success in increasing productivity and improving quality with essentially the same work force that had had a reputation for militancy and absenteeism at the previous GM plant [Weinstein, 1985].

The total value of those human resources as a group has certainly increased while the individual values may remain the same. This realization that the value of an organization's human resources may not be equivalent to the sum of the values of each employee, depending upon some factors — such as cooperation and coordination — leads to an examination of group theory with a greater interest.

Group Value of Human Resources

The group value theory, developed by Likert and Bowers, is based on the analysis of the perceived effectiveness of a group as a whole, instead of each individual. The model is analogous to the following algebraic expression:

$$Z = f(x_1) + f(x_2) + \cdots + f(x_i) + f(y_1) + f(y_2) + \cdots + f(y_i),$$

where Z, the dependent variable, is a function of both x and y. Z represents the overall productive efficiency of the organization, and is classified as the end-result variable indicating the results achieved by the organization — productivity, costs, scrap loss, growth, market share, earnings, etc. [Flamholtz, p.129].

The first category of independent variables, x_i, are the variables the organization can control in its efforts to produce the desired results. Likert and Bowers defined these independent or causal variables as managerial behavior and organizational structure. In developing the causal variables, the environment is assumed to be beyond organizational control.

The variables y_i, classified as the intervening variables, affect the end-result variables also, according to Likert and Bowers. The intervening variables are dependent on the causal variables, and represent "loyalties, attitudes, motivations, performance goals, and perceptions of all members and their collective capability for effective action, interaction, communication, and decision making."

In this model, the level of managerial commitment to promote teamwork (causal variable) would influence the amount of cooperation (intervening variable), which in turn would affect the level of productivity (end-result variable). The level of productivity is an indicator of the group value of human resources.

ILM and the Group Value Theory

When an organization has a well-developed ILM, the uncertainty of the environment — volatility in the labor market, for example — is controlled to a great extent. In a recessionary economic environment, the firm can maintain its regular work force by cutting back on part-time employees and subcontracted work. When there is a shortage of competent managers in the market also, the firm will not be affected since it will have provided for these positions through employee development.

Promoting employees from only within the organization and long-term employment, the two key characteristics of an ILM, should have positive effects on the intervening variables, y_i. Long-term employment eliminates an employee's need to protect his job by withholding information from others, and motivates each employee and department to assist one another. This is because, in the long run, their efforts will be recognized and rewarded. A higher level of cooperation leads to a better coordination, and subsequently increases productive efficiency [Ouchi, 1981].

Employees perceive job stability to be a function of the company's growth and well-being when long-term employment is provided. Hence, personal goals tend to be more congruent with the organizational goals. Goal congruency and increased employee motivation produce higher productivity.

Another major intervening variable, employee satisfaction, is enhanced by long-term employment, since it provides ample time to the managers to be aware of the needs and problems of the individuals. The long tenure also improves the performance evaluation process because the individual performance level becomes more apparent as a longer time span is used [Hatvany and Pucik, 1981].

The long tenure also increases the level of concentration on the organization's long-term objectives, since it encourages managers to avoid short-term fixes and to look at the long-term consequences. That will also reduce the fear of risk. In Chapter 2 we observed that the emphasis on a short-term evaluation process forces managers to be risk avoidant. They shun a project that is highly desirable in the long run but could jeopardize their short-term performance.

Exclusive promotion from within the organization also affects employee attitude through the development of trust between the employee and the employer and by allowing an employee to know where he stands in the organization. In companies which rely on external labor markets, however, the appointment of managers from the outside can be demoralizing for those who assumed they were next in line.

ILM as an Additional Causal Variable

An HRA system that is capable of measuring the value of employees accurately can provide managers with the necessary information for effective decision making. The group value theory looks more promising in the new managerial accounting environment.

The group value model, as discussed in the above, should incorporate ILM as an additional causal variable, along with the existing two variables — managerial behavior and organizational structure. We have seen that ILM can increase the relative strengths each intervening variable has on the end-result variables.

Being able to reduce its dependency on the environment is a tremendous advantage to a company, especially when changes take place at a rapid pace in the environment. JIT helps companies reduce their dependency on the environment by responding to changes in consumer demands more rapidly. ILM has helped many large Japanese companies and American companies such as Hewlett-Packard, Inc. cope with uncertainties in the external labor markets.

7-2. JIT AND EOQ

The economic order quantity (EOQ) model, developed by F.W. Harris in 1915, is useful in establishing optimal inventory lot sizes that would minimize the combined costs of production and inventory. JIT, on the other hand, deals with zero or minimal, rather than optimal, lot sizes. Therefore, JIT offers a major challenge to EOQ.

The total annual cost of carrying inventory (TC) is expressed, according to the EOQ model, as follows:

$TC = C_1 D/Q + C_2 Q/2$, where

C_1 = Variable costs of placing a production/purchase order,

D = Annual demand for the inventory item,

Q = Inventory quantity ordered for each lot, and

C_2 = Variable costs of holding one inventory item for one year.

The optimal EOQ, q^*, is calculated from the above equation as

$q^* = \sqrt{2C_1 D/C_2}.$

The EOQ model can answer questions such as what, when, and how much to order, and what scheduling priorities to assign to machines. The EOQ is obtained at the point where holding costs (C_2) equal preparation costs (C_1).

Can the EOQ model still be consistent with the zero inventory concept of JIT? According to Sauers [1986], when preparation costs are reduced, the economic inventory level moves toward zero. Attempting to minimize the total cost, TC, by matching holding costs with preparation costs, Sauers states, and by driving preparation costs toward zero is to have zero holding costs and zero inventories.

What the above theoretical explanations really amount to is that when minimal inventory levels are achieved by JIT, the EOQ model loses its practical usefulness, despite its elegant approach.

7-3. THE IMPACT ON CAPITAL BUDGETING

As the new environment embraces more diversified and complex manufacturing objectives — better product quality, increased flexibility, lower inventory levels, shorter lead time, etc. — the need to recognize these objectives in capital budgeting analyses becomes evident. In this section, we will look at the impacts of the changing environment on capital budgeting processes.

Hurdle Rate

The hurdle rates many U.S. companies use in the evaluation of new investment projects, according to Kaplan [1986], are 15 percent or higher, which is unrealistic. Kaplan provides the following justification for the use of a lower hurdle rate.

From 1926 to 1984 the average total return from investments in common stocks was 11.7 percent per year. The real return after inflation was about 8.5 percent per year. These historical estimates are, nevertheless, overestimates of the weighted average cost of equity and debt financing, which should be lower than the equity financing rate. Even with the recent increases in the real interest rate, a more realistic rate (weighted average) is estimated to be less than 8 percent.

Two conceptual errors, Kaplan argues, have led many corporate executives to believe their real cost of capital is higher.

First, executives use the accounting return on investment — net income/net invested capital — as a guideline in estimating their current cost of capital. The accounting ROI, however, is distorted by financial accounting conventions such as depreciation method, and by management's failure to adjust the net income and the invested capital figures for the effects of inflation.

The second conceptual error that makes executives use high hurdle rates is implicitly to compare the rates to the current market interest rates and returns on common stocks. These rates really include expectations of current and future inflation. It is inconsistent to assume a high inflation rate for hurdle rate, while a zero rate of price increase is used to estimate future cash flows from an investment.

Therefore, a lower hurdle rate is justified based on the above analysis. This is especially true if the new investment involves the installation of FMS or CIM. The new technologies will enable companies to turn out products which are of better quality with fewer rejects and recalls, thereby reducing the risk in the product output and the investment project itself.

The Correct Alternative to the Investment in New Technologies

Many investments in new process technologies such as FMS and CIM are not justified, according to Kaplan, because they are measured against a status quo alternative of making no new investments. The alternative assumes a continuation of existing market share and same level of cash flows. The status quo rarely lasts, and is an incorrect alternative.

The correct alternative, Kaplan states, should assume shrinking market share and cash flows. This is because, once a valuable new process technology becomes available, at least some competitors will invest in it. The company which decides not to invest in it will pay for it by losing competitive strength.

Longer Useful Life is Penalized

When discounted cash flow techniques are used for the evaluation of investment in new technologies, there is another built-in bias against the investment. The greater flexibility of FMS and CIM technologies allows them to be employed for successive generations of products, providing a longer useful life than conventional process investments.

The overestimated hurdle rate penalizes the investment in new technologies, which has a longer project life, more severely than other investments with shorter lives. This is because compounding effect of high discount rates will be applied more strongly to cash flows of the distant future [Kaplan, 1986].

New Elements to be Considered

Traditional capital budgeting analyses usually consider only operating cost savings, labor cost in particular, in the estimate of future cash inflows. There are many other benefits to consider, in addition to the above, in the evaluation of investment in new technologies. Kaplan has proposed to incorporate the following benefits into the analysis:

1. *Inventory savings.* Work-in-process and finished-goods inventory levels are reduced substantially due to the increased flexibility, more stable product flow, better quality, and improved production scheduling. When the new process becomes operational, there will be large cash savings as a result.
2. *Less floor space.* As computer-controlled machines replace conventional machines and the need for the storage space for inventory is reduced, a significant amount of floor space will be released because less computer-controlled machines will be necessary.
3. *Better quality.* The new technology improves the company's ability to conform to product specifications, reducing defects and increasing uniformity in products.
4. *Increased flexibility.* The same equipment will handle both current high-volume models and discontinued models; machines can serve as backups for each other; and they can easily accommodate product changes.
5. *Shorter lead time.* The new technology allows the company to respond to customer demands more quickly.

6. *Gaining experience with the technology.* This will enable managers and employees to be in a better position to deal with any future technological advances which may drastically alter the market situation.

The first three are tangible benefits while the last three are intangible. Kaplan suggests that companies try to incorporate the above benefits in the evaluation of investments. After the more easily quantified benefits have been incorporated, a resulting net present value which is positive and satisfactory to management would be considered good. If a negative net present value is obtained, it should be compared to the intangible or hard-to-quantify benefits. Management can weigh the importance of investing in automation expressed in terms of benefits against a negative NPV.

Further Considerations

Some other factors have been identified and reported on the implications of making investments in new technologies. When a small metal products company in Boston introduced a robot in the manufacturing process, a comprehensive review of the production process was forced, leading to significant product modifications. This generated large savings for the company. An additional benefit was that the visibility and credibility of a larger company was accorded by the robotics, which increased sales [Greenberg, 1986].

7-4. MANAGERIAL ACCOUNTING CHANGES FOR THE 1990s: A SUMMARY

As international influences (see Chapter 3) and technological advances (see Chapter 4) change the environment of managerial decision making considerably, managerial accounting systems need to be updated and modified to accommodate the new, different informational needs of managers.

The following is a summary of the expected changes in managerial accounting for the 1990s:

Job order costing. In a flexible manufacturing environment, workers and materials are frequently transferred between job orders. This will disrupt the accounting department's attempt to trace the costs of three elements to different job orders. Job orders, the primary scheduling and cost-tracking tool in a traditional environment, become less useful in the new setting, where lot sizes become too small to have a unique job order attached to each lot.

As the levels of work-in-process and finished-goods inventory are reduced substantially, the need to separately allocate costs to ending inventories decreases. Some companies already charge direct labor and factory overhead to the cost of goods sold directly. If some adjustments to the calculated costs are made to the satisfaction of the management and regulatory authorities, the substantial reduction in accounting costs overrides the marginal decrease in the accuracy of the calculated costs for these companies.

Process costing. The insignificant inventory levels would make the difference between the "units completed" and the "amount of work done in the current period", the elements used to calculate equivalent units in process costing procedures, very small. Accordingly, accountants could forgo the calculation of equivalent units entirely. This will save a tremendous amount of time and cost in the areas of data collection, analysis, and reporting, while the sacrifice in the accuracy of reported data would be marginal.

When JIT is implemented, a job-shop system changes to a process system: Almost zero inventory between operations; zero time between operations; and simplification of the entire process. Accountants are then dealing with process costing, rather than job-shop costing.

As JIT and total quality control concepts are successfully practiced and the spoilage and defect rates are substantially reduced, the need for a separate tracing and accounting for the costs of spoilage in process costing may become no longer essential. Instead of the concepts of normal and abnormal spoilage, all spoilage might be considered abnormal and controllable. The system would no longer tolerate normal spoilage.

Changing cost structure. The existing cost and managerial accounting systems were designed several decades ago to closely monitor direct labor costs for mass production of a few standardized items, since direct labor cost was a significant portion of total product cost.

Manufacturing overhead costs, under those systems, are allocated primarily based on direct labor costs. Since the 1920s, automation has decreased direct labor content in the production dramatically, to only about one-fifth of overhead in most firms. Management accountants must adapt to the changing cost structure.

At some companies direct labor is no longer accounted for as a separate product cost. With only 3-5% of product cost attributed to the direct labor component, accountants and managers see little benefit in standard cost and variance analyses of direct labor. Direct labor is now included in manufacturing overhead at those companies. This adjustment to the changing nature of operations will reduce a significant amount of cost and effort spent on distinguishing between the two cost categories.

JIT and cost system modification. Present cost accounting systems are too restrictive and complex to be of any value to JIT implementation. The system needs to be modified so that it will be more flexible and simple. Before any modification is made, however, there should be an internal audit of the existing cost system for proper evaluation of the new demands and current capabilities.

JIT and inventory valuation. In traditional cost systems, inventory valuation is a major task which requires a substantial amount of time and clerical cost. As JIT simplifies various phases of the firm operations, the number of transactions decreases and inventory level is reduced. Inventory valuation, accordingly, can be simplified to a great extent.

Variable costing vs. absorption costing. The changes in the environment have made variable costing less important. This is because the percentage of variable costs in the total manufacturing costs has decreased, and grouping fixed overhead items together to be charged to the period does not help the company find ways to control rising fixed overhead costs. Labor cost in an automated manufacturing system tends to become mostly fixed. In the new environment, absorption costing becomes the only meaningful costing method.

Cost collection in the new environment. Changes in manufacturing technology have made cost collection easier. The cost of acquiring data is substantially reduced as the new technologies are introduced into the system.

Knowledge workers and learning curves. As technological changes take place, knowledge workers will replace the conventional work force. Although this type of labor is more of a direct nature than indirect, it is primarily fixed. The birth of a whole new breed of professionals raises issues of motivation and performance measurement. The new technologies alter the concept of learning curves as well. The curve no longer has any significance at the machine level in an FMS or CIM setting. The reduction in labor hours of workers ceases to be an important issue.

The new environment and service industry. In the old regulated environment, firms in various service industries priced their services on the basis of all the costs incurred plus markup. A detailed analysis of costs and prices was not necessary due to the restrictions placed on the operations by regulatory agencies. Now the fierce competition in the market forces them to look at the profitability of each service individually. The companies must re-examine their costing and pricing systems so that the systems can provide useful information for long-term as well as short-term managerial decision making.

Cost allocation in the new environment. When the pool of costs, traced to each cost center, is allocated to the products, management accountants must devise new allocation bases. The single variable - labor or machine hours - currently used by most companies should be changed to multiple variables that explain how overhead costs are actually generated. Overhead costs are not driven by labor or machine hours in most cost centers, they are generated by transactions. Homogeneous cost drivers for each set of cost pools must be found for better cost allocations.

New types of costs. Technological changes create a focused subplant with U-shaped machine cells within the plant. Those cells replace traditional production departments. Different types of costs are now identified at the plant level, at the focused subplant level, and at the cell level. The value-added concept discussed in Section 5-4 can be used to break down the overhead cost pool to examine and classify costs. The same concept is also useful in the process of finding homogeneous cost drivers previously mentioned.

Cost control in the new environment. Technological advances reduce the production cycle time, which calls for timely information to support the process. In the new manufacturing environment, most of the manufacturing data never leave the system. Increased availability and accuracy of shop-floor data should help management accountants evaluate and control many indirect costs in a direct manner. The real-time processing of information should increase the usefulness further. In order to control costs in the long run, the transactions can be eliminated, integrated, stabilized, or automated. JIT eliminates transactions. Vendor scheduling, guaranteed employment, and movement toward repetitive manufacturing stabilize transactions. Bar coding and paperless factories automate transactions.

The changing role of management accountant. While the need for better real-time information for process control demands a more active role of management accountants, extensive automation makes their traditional authority over the basic data taken away. Management accountants, however, must restate cost standards in terms of new cost allocation bases through intuitive estimate with the exception of rework and maintenance because little of the usual data for calculating standard costs is available. This difficulty is more severe in high-tech fields. Some changes such as the integration of MRP with cost accounting, in the meantime, facilitate management accountant's work.

Traditional cost accounting principles and management control in the new environment. As radical changes take place in the environment of managerial accounting, the traditional cost accounting principles sometimes are in conflict with the managerial actions required to compete in the marketplace and generate profits, as discussed in Chapter 6. This calls for a new look at efficiency and productivity. U.S. industry's frustration with the results of productivity-increasing programs has been caused originally by focusing on wrong targets — cost reduction and elimination of waste and inefficiency.

This preoccupation with efficiency and cost reductions at the expense of effectiveness forces managers to adopt short-term, operational views, which detract attention from the crucial manufacturing strategy and structure and alienate the work force. In the new environment, managers must focus on a wider set of objectives than cost and efficiency. They need to be more concerned with the issue of how to extend local productivity to global optimization of resource utilization and must make a direct connection from efficiency to effectiveness.

JIT, OPT, and efficiency. When bottlenecks exist somewhere along the process, high efficiency at local production stations leads to lower profit performance for the company as a whole under the concept of OPT. In a JIT setting, idle time of workers is not regarded as evil, but inventory is. The production function here is viewed from a perspective which is entirely different from conventional perspectives. JIT seeks a more global optimization of the production and distribution network. It avoids local optimizations that may be realized at the expense of the larger system and accepts short-term diseconomies to decrease the long-term total costs.

Automation and efficiency. Individual efficiency has very little importance in an automated plant. The costs, which used to be mainly variable, become increasingly volume and product independent. Efficiency measured by the deviations from the standards on an individual basis is not the major issue.

Positive performance. The essence of management control in the new environment should be a focus on positive performance. This reflects an explicit preference for the optimum utilization of resources for the company as a whole; for compliance with the schedule within the entire manufacturing structure; for the employees' positive contribution to the attainment of the company's goals and objectives through cooperative efforts; and for making direct and consistent connections to the company's goals when managers make decisions on operations-related actions. Effectiveness, unless proper objectives are established within the system, would not contribute positively to attaining profit goals. JIT and OPT work because they yield positive performance.

The measurement of positive performance. The emphasis in the new environment should be placed on the group performance. Conflicts among employees and processes would produce a lot more serious consequences in the new environment than it did in the conventional environment. Managers must also seek global optimization of the whole production system, and avoid a tight control over the employees and the use of short-term performance measures. Instead, companies must show concern for employees and practice it over an extended period of time.

The changing environment and human resource accounting. Being able to reduce its dependency on the environment is a tremendous advantage to a company, especially when changes take place at a rapid pace. A well-developed internal labor market decreases the company's dependency on environmental conditions. The group value theory of human resource accounting, which looks more promising in the new environment than the individual value theory, should incorporate the internal labor market as an additional causal variable.

The impact on capital budgeting. If the new investment involves the installation of FMS or CIM, the use of a hurdle rate which is lower than the present rates of around 15 percent is justified. Companies also have to measure investment in new technologies against the correct alternative of shrinking market share and cash flows rather than a status quo alternative. Finally, many new elements in addition to operating cost savings must be considered to estimate future cash inflows because new technologies provide many other benefits.

REFERENCES

Doeringer, P. and M. Piore, *Internal Labor Markets and Manpower Analysis* (Lexington, Mass.: D.C. Heath and Co., 1971).

Flamholtz, E.G., *Human Resource Accounting* (Encino, Calif.:Dickerson Publishing, 1974).

Greenberg, D., "Robotics: One Small Company's Experience," *Cost Accounting for the 90s* (Montvale, N.J.: National Association of Accountants, 1986), pp. 57-63.

Hatvany, N. and V. Pucik, "An Integrated Management System: Lessons from the Japanese Experience," *Academy of Management Review* (July 1981), pp. 469-478.

Kaplan, R.S., "Must CIM Be Justified by Faith Alone?" *Harvard Business Review* (March-April 1986), pp. 87-95.

Ouchi, W.G., "Organizational Paradigms: A Commentary on Japanese Management and Theory Z Organizations," *Organizational Dynamics* (Spring 1981), pp. 36-43.

Sauers, D.G., "Analyzing Inventory Systems," *Management Accounting* (May 1986), pp. 30-36.

Weinstein, H., "U.S. Car Workers Adapt to Japanese Style," *The Los Angeles Times* (December 22, 1985), pp. 1, 16-17.

SUGGESTED ADDITIONAL READINGS

Anderson, J.C., G.T. Milkovich, and A. Tsui, "A Model of Intra-Organizational Mobility," *Academy of Management Review* (October1981), pp. 529-538.

Hill, N. and T. Dimnik, "Cost Justifying New Technologies," *Business Quarterly* (Winter 1985), pp. 91-96.

Likert, R. and D.G. Bowers, "Improving the Accuracy of P/L Reports by Estimating the Change in Dollar Value of the Human Organization," *Michigan Business Review* (March 1973), pp. 15-24.

Index